I Spoke to an Angel

Michael McKay ~ Boston Author

Introduction

My name is Michael McKay, and I spoke to an Angel and was told to give a message to everyone who believes in a higher power. This is a very true story that happened to me.

I am writing to give everyone a message about Heaven and Earth, and why God has always sent Angels here to earth and when you die one will bring you through the valley of death.

Either you will be left in the valley of death, or you will move along with that one Angel.

After meeting this Angel a few times in my life, he informed me that my job is not a simple one. As I grew older and gather followers of God. This Angel will come with others and bring Satan and his Son to their death and bring their souls before God.

Only God can destroy an Angel. God has given Satan many chances to change here on earth, but Satan never did.

Satan himself still has the power like all the other angels did before he was kicked out of Heaven. At one time while he was serving God, he was a good Angel.

This was before God casted him and his followers to earth for trying to overthrow Gods Kingdoms.

God has given Satan many changes to change, only because God has love for all, and gives everything he creates many chances to better themselves. Humans have never gotten it right to this day.

4

When I first met him, he told me his name was Michael, King of the Arch Angels. Then said, once Satan is dead, the worlds in the universes and space will open up once again. There will be no more darkness in space as you know it.

You will see other worlds, which have other people living on them. God himself will grant him the power to bring this Evil Angel called Satan before God himself.

Once Michael does this, all his followers will die with him, even Satan's son called; the Anti-Christ will perish as well.

Then Saint Michael told me that I would suffer a long time before he returns to see me again, and it is all for a good reason. He told me to never to lose my faith and for me to await his return, and I did.

This Angel told me; earth will be no more because humans have advance beyond their need for God. He made earth for Satan and called this planet Hell; it was made to give humans a second chance not only in life but in death.

People have been back here many times before because humans cannot get it right, they keep falling under Satins temptations.

God did not make humans perfect, everyone here on earth was made to make mistakes, but they never learn from their errors in life. Everyone has a lust for greed, money, and power; they are no better than Satan.

Every soul from this planet will answer to their higher power once you die.

And you will be alone when you are judged. St. Michael told me to find twenty followers who are believers in God to help spread the word of God.

He also said; Gods has had enough from nonbelievers, and anyone who reads this novel; they should start waking others up and remind them what is in store for their futures.

Everyone on this planet must repent to God.

Then when they die their souls will stand before God, and all will be judged if they do not repent before meeting him.

This is my story.

Believe in what you read because this is the word of the God. To this day, I will never know why he ever picked me.

 I will follow through with the work he commanded me to do, and whoever reads this novel shall follow the word of God.

God loves you all, he is not a God who loves to hurt people. God is pure and kind. But he has had enough from this one planet called earth, with humans hating and killing each other and believing that money is the only God on this planet.

God has killed humans and destroyed many cities in the past, and it will happen once again.

Hate only brings strength to Satan, please don't do Satan work for him. Pray to God and let God back into your life's one again.

God gains more strength from humans praying to him. Those who lost faith in him will die along with Satan and will never see the light ever again. Everyone on this earth has "Free Will."

God gave your life, love, and happiness, and he also gave you death. You die for a reason, nobody understands this. You come into this world alone and you die alone.

Greed is human's biggest downfall; everyone is only looking after themselves, and those with a lot of money only want more. Those people who have the most should be taking care of those who have nothing.

So, answer this question for me; How much is enough? You can't put a price on your soul or God.

In today's world of technology, people with money will grow into power and feel they are Gods, it's happened many times in history.

Humans will forget like those did in the past. Life is very short, and when you die, you have to leave with the love of God in your hearts, for this is the word of the lord!

You control here on earth where you go after you die. This is why humans have had this feeling that you all have done this before, because you have.

Once you come back you must start making better choices in that life and not fall back into Satan's tricks.

Ask yourselves this one question; How many people think about God every single day? Most people only need God when a loved one dies, or you are going through bad times.

Most people think of God once a week if that.

Many people here on earth think they can fool God and just cover their tracks by thinking if they go to church once a week they will be covered, it does not work that way.

You don't have to go to church to believe in God at all, you can speak to God many times a day, when you get out of bed in the morning, before meals, walking, driving, or going to bed at night. God hears you just from one simple pray.

If you read this far in this novel, give a shout out to your higher power right now, tell him how you feel right at this moment, just talk to him like you would anyone else.

If you believe God can hear you, then go out and talk to other people about God, tell them you get this great feeling when you speak to him.

If you feel warn and your eyes tear up a little that's okay, you are waking up your emotions within your souls by letting God back into your life.

Trust me, I speak to myself many times a day, in doing this I also speak to God many times a day.

You must change the way you think, start thinking more positive and if you do this, you will find a better path in life and not follow Satan and all of his temptations.

Don't let Satan's temptation place you in the valley by yourself, break free from this evil Angle he can only trick you using temptation and greed.

Satan has no power over any human here on earth, he feeds off of your greed for money, power, hate, lust and much more. I myself have felt for these demons tricks many times in my life.

Humans have stopped believing in God and his Son Jesus. God wants everyone in this living Hell to repent each day to him, and for people to do good while on this planet, he gave us all the gifts of love, but we don't use it enough.

We are all being fooled by Satan here on earth, this evil Angel love to distract you and likes you to get mad at life, because when you get mad, you are distracted, you can't think straight, and that is when you make more mistakes.

You must "Believe" and "Forgive"

We are all going to die, this is the only sure bet that you have in life. I promise you this!

I'm here as a messenger to remind everyone that God is still alive and well. Everyone on this planet has forgotten about God, and he is not happy, if you do not believe this, then you will believe it as you are dying, it will make it easier on your soul when you die. Count on this!

God has always sent his army down to speak or to look over people here on earth, sometimes people just can't see what is in front of them.

So, before we start, let me thank you for reading this story. I want nothing from anybody, and I'm not making any money from this novel. I'm hoping my story will awaken many people.

Chapter One

Everyday humans are being tested by God on this earth for a reason. I was born in Boston, Massachusetts, in a city called Dorchester.

It was extremely hard growing up back in the days, we were poor and had nothing growing up in the ghettos, but we all got by keeping the faith.

Mainly because you had to fight for everything and anything you wanted. I came from an all-Irish section, where we all fought and played hard every day. On Saturdays you were made to go to confession.

Then on Sundays morning we all went to church as a family. Everyone was catholic where I grew up in Dorchester.

I never understood why we had to go there and listen to the same old stories from the same priest every week, reading from this one book called the Bible.

Only time I ever liked church was when the priest told a story about life itself or what was happening throughout Boston.

I did like to look at the statues and the stained-glass windows in the church. I looked at every one of them each week.

I thought at an early age how wonderful these large figurines looked and wondered how someone could make such large, wonderful statues.

There was this one statue I could not get out of my head. It was of Saint Michael, who had the same name as I did.

I remembered when I was in second grade in catholic school, most of the nuns back in those days who had to deal with me, hated me out of everyone in their school.

Every few days I was sent over to the head nun, who was called Sister Superior. She would give me a slap in the face each time I was sent to her office.

Until this one day I went over to her to get my punished for talking back to one of the nuns. When I walked in through the door, a priest happened to be there instead of the head nun.

I had never seen him here before and I thought I was in big trouble now. He had me take a seat and asked me what I wanted to do in my life.

I told him I was not sure. He asked me if I believed in Heaven and Hell. I said, I am not sure Father.

He asked me if I listened to the priest while I was in Church? I said only to the stories the priest tells, and make people laugh.

He then asked me what I did when I sat in the church. I told him I loved to look at all the Angels of the statues inside there. Then he asked me, which one was my favorite?

I told him Saint Michael, and I perked right up. He told me that was his favorite as well and told me his name was Michael as well.

He then asked me if I knew anything about Saint Michael. I told him we had the same name.

He smiled as he looked into my eyes and started to tell me all about Saint Michael who cast Lucifer and other Angels and Demons out from Heaven when a war broke out.

Because all those bad angels that rebelled against God as you know him to be, were judged to be cast out of Heaven onto earth.

God called Lucifer by a new name which was "The Devil" and all those other angels who followed Lucifer were called demons.

They were sent out of Heaven with Lucifer. God is known by many names from people of many different religions; I knew him as God.

Lucifer is called by many names he told me, but he is the Devil. He is evil and an unbelievably bad Angel.

He still has powers which many angels have, but God has the most power.

This left me a little confused. Because I thought if God were so powerful and the big boss, why could not he just snap his finger and make them all go away.

Father Michael told me I will learn more as I grew and keep going to classes and educate myself.

Then he told me Saint Michael was God's right-handed Angel, and Saint Michael controlled all the angels in Heaven and when each human dies one angels will walk each soul to meet God, and each soul will be judged.

Father Michael smiled at me then said; We will meet again, and for me to wait for the head nun to come in and as he walked away, he walked out and closed the door, and it slammed hard.

Then the head nun came in from the other room.

She asked me what took me so long for me to get there, and why I had to slam the door in her office?

I told her I had been here for twenty minutes, and I did not slam the door Father Michael did. She slapped me in the face for lying to her, I told her she can go ask the new priest.

She said we do not have any new priest here. I told her I just spoke to him for all the time I was here.

She yelled at me and said stop it, stop lying. I just heard you slam the door close. I was right in the other room she yelled.

I saw you come in and sit down. I told her she was wrong, and I was talking to Father Michael. She slapped me once again and told me to stop making up stories.

She then told me I would be leaving this school and going into public school, because she had enough of me.

I hated her and all the other nuns there; they even kept me back in the second grade. My mom was not that happy either and she beat me all the way home.

When Sunday came around, I wanted to see this new priest, just to show my mother and everyone I was not lying. I went to church and the same old priest was up their talking.

After the Mass was over, I walked up to the priest and asked him where Father Michael was? He looked at me with a strange look and told me there were no new priest there at all and none by that name.

I told him I met Father Michael, then looked down to my feet. I was confused and did not understand what was going on, I knew I spoke to somebody that day.

Nobody believed me at all, and I did not understand any of it. I was like anyone else from my Irish neighborhood. Where I grew up you became a police officer, a criminal, or a priest.

I was a kid that had a good relationship with everyone. I was always that quiet kid that would just listen to everyone's stories and smiled.

I liked playing street hockey or stick ball and every one of us got into some kind of trouble back in the day.

If a police officer caught you doing something wrong, he would kick your butt right there on the spot, and you took it like a man because everyone would be watching.

That was just how things were back in my earlier days. Even teachers would send you down to the gym teacher to get an ass whipping if you were disrespectful.

Nobody ran home and told your mom what happened, because you would get another beating for telling.

My older brothers were always in trouble for some reason. I remember when the Beatles came to this country and my older brothers would wear Beatle boots with pointed toes and slick back their hair with vaseline.

I was the second youngest out eight kids, and I always was the one to get my older brothers hand me downs and got pushed around the most. It was not easy being me as a kid.

Chapter Two

It was summertime and I was about thirteen years of age; my brother Raymond called me up. He was living up north and asked me if I wanted to come up there for a visit and he would give me my own apartment until I was ready to return to Boston back to school.

My mom was behind it because she did not like the kids I was hanging around with. I was turning into a teenager, and our country was going through many things back in 1968.

I took a bus ride up to north, what a long ride it was going up there. It took about three days. Back then, it was extremely hot on those buses, they did not have air conditioners when I was a kid.

I just smoked my weed and slept for the whole ride up there. My brother Raymond picked me up at the bus station and he was telling me how great it was there.

He told me it was good I came there in the summertime and not in the winter because it was much colder than Boston. He told me I could piss out ice cubes because it was so cold there.

I lived in Boston, and I was used to the cold. But people from Boston had nothing on these people that live up there near the Canada border from what my brother told me.

My bother hooked me up with my own apartment.

I was one floor above him, and I helped him with work within the building. I met some kids a little older than me and a few my own age, his name was Emmet.

This one kid and I got along very well, and we hung together every day when I was done with my job. The first time we met, I was joking around with the way he spoke. He was from Oklahoma, and he had a deep midwestern accent.

Funny thing was, he uses to make fun of my Boston accent as well. It was nice to have someone to hang out with and try to pick up girls and laugh with.

I remember in 1963 John F. Kennedy our President from Massachusetts was murdered.

I remembered that one day everyone in the streets was crying. People were incredibly sad from this one man being murdered. I was only in third grade when I first heard of it. I felt bad about this one great man everyone loved. By 1968 many things were happening in our country.

Black people and whites were fighting and killing each other. After Martin Luther King was murdered, riots broke out everywhere.

Then another Kennedy was shot and killed. Back in my days everyone was rioting about something. But most people were fighting our government over the Vietnam war.

Three great men were murdered in the 1960's and people cried and lined the streets for Martin Luther King Jr and Bobby Kennedy. I thought to myself why people on this earth would hurt such kind men.

There was a big movement going on within this country. Drugs were big back in those days. Me, I stayed with smoking pot and drinking beer.

Back in Boston I went to school whenever I felt like it, I figured that the streets could teach me everything I wanted to know back in those days.

Most people were all drugged up, we had the hippy movement going on, most people had long hair, and we all wore bell bottom pants.

To me, it seemed like the entire world was stoned out of their minds. I remember my brother asked me what I wanted to do with my life.

I told him I wanted to go into the military once I turned eighteen. This was my only goal in my life. I wanted to join the Navy.

Back in South Boston. I used to go to the Fargo Building and became a Sea Cadet. I loved it, and it gave me something to look forward to every week, we would march in parades and go on real navy ships.

I was the only one that did not have a uniform, because we were poor.

They let me stay as a cadet without a uniform, because there was this one guy who was an Admiral who ran everything there and we got along very well.

He would even drive me from the Fargo building to the bus station to go home once a week. At first, I did not know how high of a rank this one man had. Then I found out, and I was shocked.

I used to walk anywhere in the building with him, and everyone would move out of his way and stand at attention and salute him. I thought to myself that this was very cool.

I was extremely impressed and loved walking around with him. He was an old man in his late forties.

I thought he had some remarkable stories to tell. We would talk all the time, but he wanted me to go to school and better myself.

I wanted to know more about him, but he never talked about wars he was in. I never understood why until I grew older.

He was one of the greatest men I ever met in my life. I did try to join the Boy scouts in Dorchester, but they threw me out because I did not go along with their program, to me, they were boring.

My new friend asked me if I wanted to take a ride down to Oklahoma with him and I said, "sure, why not. I told my brother I would be back in a week or so, he told me to be careful.

Emmet told me when I got down there, I could get my driving license down there because the age back then was younger than most states. I drove anyway without a license anytime I wanted if someone would let me borrow a car.

Emmet said we would take turns driving so we could get down there quicker, and that is what we did. Once we got down there, I met his uncle, and Emmet gave him the keys to the car we drove down there.

Then his uncle gave him money and Emmet gave me half the money his uncle gave him.

I could not figure out why he was giving me half the money for his car. Then he told me he stole cars and brings them back and forth.

We slept at Emmet's house in a town called Edmond. He had a house full of girls. I also could not believe it when he was going out with one of his cousins. Somehow, that was just so wrong, yet none of his family cared about it.

We stayed there for a few days. I did not like it much because you could not buy any real beer or liquor. They sold beer in supermarkets with less than the alcohol most states gave you.

If you wanted a drink, we had to drive up to the hills and buy moonshine. There was no way this city boy was ever going up those hills. I did go up received my driving licenses when I was there.

I asked Emmet how we are going to get back to Minnesota. He told me his uncle was going to give us a car to bring back. I said that is cool, I then asked him why he gave me all that money from his uncle.

Then he told me that we will bring another one back to Minnesota and get some more money. He asked me if I had a problem with that, I told him no, not at all. I could not believe the money they paid us.

Then I started thinking there had to be drugs in these cars as well. I was from Boston and was not that stupid. Then we would get the same amount when we bring another one back.

I knew that when I returned up north, I was not going to do this anymore because I wanted to make it back to Boston with my other friends and did not want to go to jail up there.

So, after a few days we got into another car, and we headed back. It took us two days to get back there, and I got paid another $350.00.

I headed back over to my brothers' apartment, and he asked where I had been, he said you have been gone over a week?

I told him I had a chance to make some good money and gave him five hundred from the seven I made. He said to me. Michael, I do not need any trouble up here from the police.

I told him not to worry, and that I am not going anymore. He thanked me for the money. He laughed and said that was more than he made for working at the apartment buildings per week. But he also had free rent, he had two kids at the time so, I knew he needed the money.

Chapter Three

Emmet showed up a few days later and asked me to take a ride with him, and I did. We went to this car dealership, and we went in and looked around and asked to take a car for a test drive.

Back then you just wrote out a two-hundred-dollar check, and they gave you the keys. So, we took this 1968 GTO fully loaded and drove around and stopped at a hardware store and had a copy of the key made.

I asked Emmet, "what are you up to? He said this is how we steal cars up here.

I told him back in Boston, people just used dent-pullers. He told me he would wait a couple of days and go back and get the car and make more money.

He told me he made more than $700.00 a week doing it this way if he drove them back down to his uncle. I was impressed with the money he made, and it was so easy to do.

We drove the car back and told the dealership and he told them he would think about buying it, and we left. Emmet asked me if I wanted to make some more money. I asked; What do you want done?

He told me tomorrow night I will drive you back to the dealership, and you take this key and drive it off the lot, and you follow me in this car.

I asked him how much I would make. He said $200.00. I said make it Three hundred, he said okay. Then I told him this would be the last one because I promised my brother, I would not get in trouble up here.

I also said I am not going back with you to your uncle's place in Oklahoma. Because I am heading back to Boston in a week or so.

He agreed and told me we will stay in touch with each other.

It was Saturday night, and we drove up to the dealership. I got out and walked over to the car and unlocked it and started it up, it was a very loud car.

I drove it over to the exit and there was this heavy chain blocking the cars in the lot. All I could do was floor it, hoping it would break the chain, and it snapped it.

I drove out of there so fast; Emmet could not even catch up with me, I started laughing. I took the car over to my brother's apartment building and parked it there and waited.

I figured Emmet would come over there to meet me. He never showed up.

The very next morning I reached him by phone. I asked him what happened and why he could not catch up with me.

He laughed and said the car was too fast, and because he was driving another stolen car, he did not want to get in trouble by the police that late at night.

 I asked him if he was going to pick up this car. He asked me to bring it over there and he would pay me; I told him I would.

I just wanted my money to be done with this car stuff. I remember having lunch with my brother telling him I would be back in an hour or so.

I left and got into the GTO to bring to Emmet. I started driving up this main road and I was in traffic at a   red light.

I looked over to my right and there was a guy getting out of a mustang yelling over at me. I leaned over to my left because I could not hear what he was saying to me because the car was loud.

I then shut it off, so I could hear what he was saying. He was telling Cody that it was his car, and it was stolen from his car lot last night.

He then told me if I pulled it over and gave it back to him, he would give me some money, and not tell the police, all he wanted was his car back.

I thought about it for a second, then for some reason in my mind, I could not let that happen. I started the car up and drove it right up to the other side of oncoming traffic. I looked into the back mirror, and he was trying to catch up with me.

But the car I was driving was much faster than what he was driving. I was taking lefts and rights and on a straight away, I was flying. I could tell he was not giving up. I could not believe this was happening to me.

I was on these two miles straight away, flooring it. Then I shifted down a couple of gears and the car started fish tailing when I took this left turn about 35mph then flooring it as it straighten out. I looked up and there was a tractor trailer truck blocking the street unloading its cargo.

All I remember doing was reaching for the handle to jump out of the car. I remember the door opening and the door hitting a parked car, then I went into a daze.

I opened my eyes, and I was being held by something or somebody. I looked into its eyes, and it was talking to me without moving his lips. We both were communicating through each other's minds, it felt like all time had come to a stop.

He asks me, "do you remember me, Michael? I thought to myself and said, "You are Father Michael whom I met when I was in sister superiors office.

Yes, we spoke then Michael. I told him nobody ever heard of you in that church, he smiled at me and told me he was Michael of the Archangels.

I asked him if I was dead. He said no, not yet. He had this soft gentle smile as I communicated with him. We were having Synchronicity.

He told me God ordered him to find one person on earth that could get a message out in this world to those who stilled believed in him. I asked him how could someone like me do this for God.

He smiled towards me and said, When this time comes, you will do this without question and while I was still alive here on earth, I would serve God.

He told me as I grew older, I would suffer very much while living here on earth and would do terrible things while I was alive. I remembered word for word what he said to me.

Then he said to me: Remember when we talked about Satan? I said yes.

Remember he is your enemy and not your friend, he could be right beside you and could be one of the closest people you trust in life here on earth.

He will know you and I have spoken; he still has that power of an Angel. He will try to get you to join him while you are here in this place, they call earth. I want you to join him and just be yourself.

You might even forget what we talked about, but as you grow, it will all come back to you, and you will become much stronger.

You yourself will be given a gift from the high Heavens. There are many ways to fool Satan. He never looks at the big picture, only things happening now.

Everything in this world will change as you grows stronger, Satan has a son called the Antichrist. They both live off the souls of hate from humans they both deceive on this earth. This must happen, he told me.

When peoples souls leaves their shell, Angels take their souls to meet God, and they will be judged. I asked; Do you mean God himself? Again, he smiled, then told me; God is the one person who can judge all, and he is called "God" for a reason.

Many people have many different names for him while praying to him. It is called nondenominational in your language. There are many different religions on this planet and God is fine with that.

What people do in this place of the living will depend on how and where you will end up when your shell is empty.

God lives off the strength from people praying to him. Those lost humans must look at the bigger picture while they are living on this earth, they all must start repenting and be sincere, and give their whole mind and body to God and his son Jesus.

I am telling you this because when it is your turn to meet him, you will understand him as "The Almighty" and no other name.

Everyone who believes or does not believe in him will meet him. This is why everyone fears death he said, it's the unknown certainties about life, and death is part of life.

God already knows you, and what you are going to do for him. This earth, and those who believe in a higher power, will know God made it happen, and it was done for the good of all.

Everyone has been evaluated until the end of their time on this earth. Satan will be defeated here on earth when it is time.

The universe will then open once again.

I then asked Saint Michael: Is earth Hell? Again, he smiled at me and did not answer my question. Then said to me he will see me in the years to come, and until then.

They will be watching over me from the Heavens above. But, I have so many questions for you, I said to him.

He then said, I will give you all the answers to your questions once we meet again. You will have to decide what questions you need answers.

Remember there are nonbelievers and true believers. True believers will help you out without question.

When this happens, you will start to spread the word of God. He then told me to remember what we spoke about. You will have this one gift from God as you grow, you will see what will happen in the future and more. Use it wisely .

Do not tell anyone about your gift or us meeting until we meet again, as you grow older Satan will come to you, give him what he wants, and do whatever he wants.

He will evaluate you and temp you with many things. I am going to put you down now Michael. I will return to talk to you again when you become 65 years old in your time. Fifty years from now in your 2020. The world will become complicated at that time.

I will bring a message for you to tell the world from God himself. After you do this, only then I will walk your soul through the valley to meet God himself.

Over these many years you will be overwhelmed with hate. But when we meet again you will be older and smarter and you will tell people the truth on how we met, and what to call their God they believe in.

They all know there can be only one God. God hears all from those who pray and believe.

Only he will walk me thought the shadow of death to meet God. I was to never speak about this to anyone until we meet again. He asked, will you do this for me Michael? I told him I would.

The last words he said to me was, do not thank me yet, for you have no idea how much you will suffer while you are alive here on earth. Then in a loud voice he yelled out; "For you will Hate me before you're done living

Chapter Four

Then out of nowhere, I felt myself rolling in the grass and heard this large crash. I jumped onto my feet and seen that GTO crashed into the truck, my right shoulder hurts.

I thought the car was going to blow up. I ran past the car door lying on the ground, and I ran one block over to a girl's house I knew and told her I had just wrecked a car. She and her brothers ran over to see the crashed car and see what was happening.

They came back and told me the engine went right through the front seats of that car after impact and the car door broke off after it hit a parked car.

They looked at me trying to figure out how I survived that crash. I told her I jumped out before I hit the truck and only hurt my shoulder a little bit.

They gave me some ice for my shoulder. Then he asked me how I could have jumped from the car, which was on the street moving fast, all the way onto the grass over the sidewalk.

They could not fathom how I ever got out of that car. They were happy I was alive and did not die that day. They never understood how I did not die.

They drove me over to my brothers and I called Emmet and told him I got chased and crashed the car.

He did not care, he said he will get another one this week. I told him I am heading back to Boston, and I will stay in touch with him.

He wished me good luck and hoped to meet me again when I visited again. I spoke to my brother and told him I needed to get back to Boston and told him I wanted to fly this time.

I paid for my ticket and thanked him very much and I told him I will be back again someday. He thanked me for coming up and hopes to see him again.

As I was on the plane returning to Boston, I kept going over in my mind on what that Angel told me. Then I thought it was just my imagination running wild.

I kept thinking it had to be true, because it was the same person I met dressed as a priest.

This time he was not dressed as a priest; he held me in his arms and covered me. I remember seeing his face being tucked inside of this light and all I could see was his face glowing.

I tried to understand how we could have had such a long discussion, without moving our lips. It was like we were speaking to each other's brain, but it was only seconds.

And then he told me I will meet him once again, when I reached the age of sixty-five. I thought that was really a long time away, and I would be incredibly old.

I was so apprehensive and felt a little delusional about believing what had just happened to me.

I asked myself. Why me? They had to be better people around to do this than me. I am a nobody, and I am just a kid. I am not that great of a person. I am troubled and people hated me because I was an evil little shit.

I then thought if I told anyone what had happened, nobody would ever believe me at all.

I then smiled and thought if I told my mother she would put and ass whipping on me for making something like this up. She and my father were very religious. We landed in Boston; all I could think about was what happened with that car wreck.

I really wonder if this were true, how could I ever tell everyone in this world. I could never tell anyone what happened, they would lock me up in an institution.

Then I tried not to think about it.

When I returned to Boston, I met up with my good friend Mikey, we have been friends since the age ten. I could not ever find a better friend than Mikey.

I was from Dorchester, and he was from a town over called Southie. I forget even how we met, but we did, and we did some unbelievably terrible things in life.

When we were together, everyone knew something bad was going to happen. It was just how things were back in the days. I thought to myself if anyone was Satan it was Mikey.

When he and I would drink beers and kick back, I used to look at him and start laughing at him. He would ask me what is so funny? I told him you are the devil the way you acted around people.

You love hurting people, I said. He said to me sometimes he felt like Satan most of the time, and we both laughed. It brought me to tears laughing so hard because I really thought he was Satan.

When I went to bed at night. I would talk and fight within my own mind about this event ever happening. I always tried to talk myself out of what happened, and I refused to accept an empirically verifiable reality; I was in total denial.

This is considered one of the most basic defense mechanisms, as it is typical of early childhood development. I convinced myself that this event did not occur.

I grew up never believing in God or whatever Saint Michael called him. I started to get so angry at myself, because I could not understand within my own mind what had happened that day.

I did not want to believe it happened. It ate at me each day, until I fought it off by doing terrible things and staying high and angry.

I was a kid who never even went to church, because I was a street kid at an early age.

As I got older, I had two kids, and I refused to take them into any church because I did not want what happened to me to happen to them. I did not want to corrupt their minds.

I just did not understand what happened or why it happened to me. I do know something saved me that day from not dying. I remember it like it happened yesterday when I met Saint Michael twice.

Then I thought about what he told me about meeting Satan. Something happened to me that made me so angry.

Why, I thought to myself. I started to deny everything that happened, I started thinking Satan was my head.

Saint Michael did tell me he had powers, and he wanted me to collaborate with him.

He told me Satan would know that Saint Michael spoke to me, and he would change me, because he loves taking on all challenges from Saint Michael and anyone who collaborated with him. He wanted me to do the work of Satan until he returned to me.

It seemed to me that the more I thought about it, the more I learned how to control it. After a while, I just took life a day at a time, and I told myself I would wait for that one day to come when Saint Michael would come back to me and tell me more.

And if he did not come back, then I would know it was the hard fall I took that day on the grass.

Then that raised another question in my mind, there was no way I could have landed on that grass without help. If I jumped, I would have hit the sidewalk, or the car door would have hit me as I was jumping out.

Either way I should have been killed that day or got hurt badly from the speed of the car. I came to one conclusion many years after fighting within my mind about this one subject.

For every reason in my mind, I could think of, on why it did happen, there was no better reason on why this did not happen to me.

I stayed with my true beliefs that God never existed. I lived my life and waited to see if St. Michael would return. I remember him telling me just to be myself, and he was still looking out for me. As I grew each year, things were very bad for me.

I learned that Saint Michael was right. I am doing badly, and I am suffering, but I thought it could not get any lower than how I am living my life right now.

I was about seventeen years old and thought I could do anything I wanted; I was wrong. I suffered for more than eighteen years. I cursed Saint Michael and God each day.

People thought I was crazy when I looked up to the sky, holding my fist up using every curse word I could think of and curse God

Chapter Five

As I grew up as a kid, my life went downhill, as each decade went by. I could not wait to see if I would make it until I was sixty-five years old.

As my life went on each day and weeks at a time. I still cursed at God up there thinking they were looking down at me laughing.

I did start to understand when he told me how I would suffer while I was living. He was right.

I went through hell as I knew it, I suffered each day with body pain throughout my body. Once I turned the curtain age of thirty-three, I felt like the world came down upon me.

I also understood that when Michael the Angel told me I would remember more from meeting him as I grew older. I would remember more about pain and suffering, and that is what happened.

As I was getting older, I started to see the future in many of my dreams.

At this time in my life, I had power like no other human could imagine. It all started happening by me seeing many things in my dreams at first, but then my dreams started coming true, and this started to freak me out.

As I learned to deal with seeing the future, all my friends around me started to die. People I knew for eighteen or forty years were just dying around me.

I knew when they were going to die. I wished I could have told them, but something inside of me would not allow me to do this.

Until now here in 2025. I have the power of shaking a hand or looking into someone's eyes and knowing when they will die soon. This is why I try very hard not to touch anybody or shake their hands.

I started to get this gift when I became thirty five years old. It took years before I knew what power I had. I knew things that nobody else knew.

I always knew when something bad was going to happen as well. The visions of the future were in my thoughts when I slept or dreamed. I started to see the future of this world in a unique perspective than most humans did here on earth.

I had something that most people would call a sixth since. It was more than that, and I was getting stronger and more smarter within my mind.

This feeling I had, I only spoke about it twice in telling a person not to do it or go somewhere because something bad was going to happen.

But did they listen? Nope, they learned the hard way, something bad did to them. This is when I knew I had this gift or power.

I had to believe this was what St. Michael was taking about with me having this power to see what is yet to come for humanity.

I was seeing everything clearly in my dreams and then watching the news with them speaking about what I dreamed. I still asked myself. Why me?

I saw numbers flashing before my eyes, dreaming about people being sick and dying and many more dreadful things.

I knew it all had to do with mathematics; all these numbers I was seeing was for a reason. I was fifty years old before I realized what all these numbers meant. I knew that mathematics fits into every equation in life.

Matter of fact math was my best subject in school; it's the only equation that fits into all human's ability to function. Think about this, if you bend down to pick up a paper, mathematics has everything to do with what you just done.

I dreamed of two very tall buildings falling from a big city. I remember seeing the date's 9112001 running through my brain, years earlier. I did not understand it.

I did not see what brought the buildings down. I just saw the dates and buildings falling, that is all I remember from that dream. I started to see the future of this world and what was going to happen.

I saw how this world was going to end, and how people would know and see it coming. I was scared for my family, and for my wife and my sons, and my grandson.

Yes, I know when our earth will be destroyed, and I'll pace it in this book.

More numbers kept running through my brain. 20202020. It did prove to me that this power I had, nobody else had it, and I could not tell anyone. I did not tell anyone, I try to change people's minds now, rather than later.

I could never tell anyone what I could see, not until I spoke to St. Michael once again in 2020. I waited and waited and trusted in him for that one day to come.

Before I turned sixty-five years old, I have worked for Satan and did his work for as long as I could remember.

I thought about why Saint Michael or God himself would want me to conduct this work for Satan.

Just to gain his trust, or their trust? I could say it was for the work of God, but Satan knew I spoke with St. Michael, and I did what was asked of me.

It was never written that Satan was to run hell at all. He still had power as an Angel, but he never was the ruler of hell, God runs everything still. Satan can only use temptation on all humans, which most humans can't get enough of.

He cannot take over your body and make you do something. You do it because you liked what popped into your brain at that very second. You have the choice to do it or not.

This is why when you are born onto this earth, you must make the right choices in life, then when you die, God will open his arms for you, and your soul will belong to him.

So, stop looking to hurt, or manipulate, and hate others. Start doing good things in this world and help God help you, so God can save a few humans while living on this planet.

It made me believe that there might be a more powerful being other than a Satan living on this earth which must be hell. I read the Bible and spoke to other people about their religions with what they believed in. To me it was all the same as St. Michael told me.

They all are praying to the same higher power. It didn't matter what beliefs other humans had, as long they were kind and showed love to one another.

It was strange how other people with different religions had thought. Even these phony people claiming to see God and telling their flocks that God only talks to them. How naive can people be?

Some church leaders are doing the devil's work, by stealing money from their flocks and lying to people that have exceptionally large followings.

Many of these followers are being fooled. I guess all these preachers who lie to their flock will pay for it when they must answer to God himself. Then they will finally figure it out.

I figured out who the most powerful beast on earth was. It was so easy to figure it out, and it was right in front of me all the time. It had more power than Satan. It was, "Humans living on Earth."

Satan and his other demons knew how to get into everyone's heads using temptation. Satan grew to power from all those lost souls who did his dirty work.

Satan guided them to do whatever he wanted them to do, this is how he got into my head. I allowed him to feed my head with false hopes, and it worked.

Many wars have been fought all over religion and there are no winners in war. This is why St. Michael wanted me to accept Satan. I did many bad things one human can do to another. I have killed, lied, cheated, stole in my younger days.

St. Michael wanted me to figure this out by myself before he came to see me again, and I did, I was right on the money.

Money is the root of all evil, it does not matter if it is gold, paper, or coins. Money is the only universal language in the world we live in. Now you figure out why this is to be?

Humans are only dangerous to one another. God is even mad at those who sell religion and his prayers, either on TV or in person. Humans have destroy each other along with money and technology.

Humans will break every rule on earth by stealing and hurting one another. Hate is the key word in any language people have within themselves. Many people have forgotten how to love each other.

Everyone wants to be the ruler of this hellish place called earth. But why is this? What is so important for humans to hate each other knowing that you are going to die and face God himself?

God sent Jesus here to earth to try and teach humans about love and kindness. If everyone living on this planet could get along and loved each other, we would all agree it would be a great place to live.

I would hope by me asking people to start changing their way and helping each other out, it would become contagious, and we might be able to spread the love around the globe, and no more people would suffer in life.

You cannot take wealth with you; this is a fact!

My father-in-law is well off and he is a religious man, but even though he is ninety years of age, he put money before God, he believes he can buy his way into Heaven.

What are you going to tell somebody like him? Do you believe you can lie to God, or fool him? Not going to happen to people!

Money is the root of all evil on this planet which I have written a few times. Hate is growing more now than ever before.

People should be praying or speaking to God more. Satanic followers are people like you and me. We have fell into Satan games believing we are serving him in a good way, they believe he is good, and God is bad.

Satan is real, and he is here on earth to corrupt people's minds, again, it only makes him more powerful.

Satan helps creates leaders all over the world, then places them in power, who then starts wars, they control other humans who murder each other, and it causes more bitterness and chaos amongst humans.

Once people are consumed with hate, and they get confused. Most humans never understand what is going on in life and God can only hope they can learn about after death.

People work hard to take care of their families and live for the love of their children; they can never get ahead in life.

They are all too busy being puppets for Satan, this is the year 2025.

Yes, I spoke with Michael once again in 2020. He returned to me just like he said he would. I was in shock when he appeared before me once again. My room in my house got bright and all I could do was fall to my knees.

I looked up to him and asked him one question. I asked him why 2020 was the most important year for him to come to see me. He told me this is the year everything will start; it was meant to happen this year.

He said to me; Think of those numbers you have seen these in your dreams, Yes, I said. Then you know what needs to be done starting this year 2020 St. Michael said to me.

God and his son have sat back and watched humans kill each other for many "Centuries" and "Millenniums." Over either land, food or what you call money.

All these wars God has watched happen from this one planet has brought him much sadness. Many of these battles before they started, both sides would bend on their knees praying up to him for strength St. Michael told me. God could not believe this.

They wanted his blessing to go kill another human being. God knows they were all followers from their leaders of each country. God only shook his head, he could not believe humans could be so addicted to violence and believe they were doing the right thing by going to war killing each other.

They used massive bombs by killing the innocent each day. God looks over the people in this world and watches how everyone acts.

I am just going to tell you the truth. God is not happy, and he has had enough from humans here on earth.

Chapter Six

People prayed to God in hopes he would look after them while they killed each other, this made God even angrier. God knew that humans did not understand his rules because Satan was behind all of this.

Saint Michael told me the first person ever to die was a person killed by a stone from another human. This made God incredibly angry over the years as he pondered over it.

God sat and watched as more people started to hate and hurt each other. God commanded Saint Michael to have one of his Angels cast a stone to earth to teach humans they cannot act out like this.

God hopes this will bring peace once again, for those who survived this rock which was tossed to earth, they would all have to start over once again.

Michael did what God had ordered. An Angel cast a stone through the universe, and it hit Earth, and took out most of humanity completely.

This has been done three other times, and the final one will be the last one. People will know it is coming this time because God wants them to feel the "fear" in their souls knowing they cannot be saved.

He wanted everyone to know what will be coming this time because they either can fall with Satan or be with him in Heaven. Then and only then they have only one choice.

God knows how to place fear into the heart of humans, they will either get on their knees and pray and repent for all their sin or believe their governments can stop this rock coming to earth.

Once they see this rock and it hits earth, another will follow right behind it with Saint Michael leading the charge.

Angels will collect all the bad souls and leave them in the valley, and after defeating Satan for good. St. Michael will hand Satan's and his Son souls to God. Because only God can kill an angel.

Religion should be free to speak about God. Some religions milk money from their flock and become very rich to hold onto power.

Their greed is overwhelming; their followers do whatever they say. This is so wrong at every level.

The leaders from some of these religious groups sit back and watch other humans suffer as their wealth grows, which makes them more powerful over time. They do not help the poor and the weak, they are full of greed. Some of them are "Demons who work for Satan."

Those few leaders of some of these churches who have very little money and believe in God, cannot do enough for the people who believe in God.

Saint Michael told me; These leaders of churches must help their followers with whatever they need to get the word of God spoken throughout this planet.

Everyone who believes in God, will believe in you, only because you will be on this mission to serve God and share his message.

They have to understand you do not want their money or wealth; you are just a servant of God bringing them a message. There will be no negotiating, either they will help you and Gods followers, or not.

As I knelt before Saint Michael, I have suffered with more pain like no human has ever suffered before. The day I reached fifty years old, that was the day my pain and suffering was coming on more. I had no idea if Satan was doing this to me or was it a test from God.

From the age of fifty until now. I've have had more than thirty back surgeries, cancer, and bad lungs (IPF).

I just wanted to die; many doctors told me I would never live beyond five years and can't understand why I'm still living to this day. I'm still alive for others to read about my story.

Drinking and pills could not take way the pain over a long many of years since Saint Michael came to me. I asked him if he could take all my pain away? He told me yes; he could remove all my pain just as fast he stopped me from getting killed as a kid in that car.

Then he looked at me and said: I will not do this. You have a job to conduct here on this world called earth. You have sinned, and you must deal with it like Gods Son Jesus had to deal with all he went through.

God and I heard you cursing us for days at a time while you were in your room, and when you were going through tough times, and outside looking up toward the sky.

I told you I would look over you, and I told you would suffer. I asked him why I must suffer instead of just doing what you wanted.

I could do a better job if I had my strength. He told me God wanted me to understand how it was to suffer.

All the people in this world are suffering and need help, you need to feel as bad as they are feeling. Jesus suffered before he was sent to his death, then returned for all to see. This was God's greatest gift for all humans.

So, you must feel the pain of others, he told me. Satan must know your suffering and God will not help you. You will never die from the pain you are in; he told me. You will die when God is ready to take you into Heaven.

Never give up, he said to me. This is how you will fool Satan because he is quite easy to fool, because a fool cannot overcome their greed.

Many people on the place called earth has suffer and died and nobody helped them out, do you know why this is he asked.

I told him because people only want money and power, and they all are ruled by governments, and Satan has placed them all in power and some wanted to take over this world.

Just like Hitler and many like him did before. How come God or nobody in Heaven ever stopped Hitler from killing all the Jews? How come there have been so many genocides in this world from one person calling all the shots?

It was Satan dealing by giving those few humans power to know they can do this to fellow men, women, and children. Yes, you are right my son. It has been tried many times before. You will have greatness when you leave here St. Michael told me.

You will stand beside God himself and watch me slay Satan and his son and bring them before God. I will cut out his soul and hand it to God.

He then told me he would be leaving soon, and he knew that I had many questions for him. He said he would allow me to ask him any questions about my quest.

I sat in the chair trying to think of the best questions one could ever ask him. My mind was racing, and I had so many questions, but I did not know where to start. I looked at him and spoke.

"I know who controls all these governments and armies, how can I being one man defeat armies throughout this world and take down governments?

This being 2025 people have more hate in them now than ever before. Yes, he said to me, this is all part of Satan plans.

Did you understand this? Yes, I said to him. I kept seeing these numbers throughout my life, why is this?

He asked me if that was part of my questions for him? I said yes. I told you that I will give you all answers to your question once we meet again.

Think back, he said to me. I told you as you grew you will have this gift, and now you can see into the future as you grew older.

I then asked St. Michael; I had this power come over me in dreams and I knew when something was going to happen to someone or when they would die. I had visions of the world's future. I know how this world will end and when, I said to him.

I do remember seeing these numbers in my dream, was that real? He said, yes, you were given that power, just to see what you would do with it, and how you dealt with it. You did well in saving your son and friends with what you seen in your dreams.

You even seen how other people lived in other worlds of this universe. They do not fight or kill he told me.

Yes, I said, I saw many other worlds in the universes in which people love one another all the time and there were no wars. They prayed to Gods many times within their days and night and are all happy.

I then asked him; Should people fear death? His answer was, why fear the inevitable.

When authors wrote the Bible, it is written 365 times; "Don't be Afraid" in it. They were speaking about death, and it is written 114 times about "Temptation" they are speaking about being tempted by Satan.

Then I said to him; My job is to have Gods followers within all and any religions, and have them find their way back to God and to get everyone to Repent . . . Right?

Yes, you are right my son. You will conduct the word of God without question. Only good will come out of all this, once it ends. One thing you can tell everyone, my son. Tell them when they are born, that is where their journey starts in life.

When life starts for humans through birth, it's up to their parents to teach them about God. After that it is up to the children to carry on their tradition. This is not happening in today's world of humans.

The truth is: When all and any people die, it is just another journey.

It could be their final one, because there are many steps after death, they can turn to dust when Satan and his son is dead, or they can enter the next step after death. Humans never think of the after death.

There is more to life when humans control their own destiny with the love of God in their heart and soul. When they except God there is nothing to fear in life or death.

Many will laugh at you and this book your writing, and think you are ridiculous and that is okay, because this is what they all said to Jesus.

Now your time is short, you must find a way to tell everyone to find their "Faith" and start believing once again. If they do not, they will all die at once, and nothing will save anyone or anything living on this Earth.

Chapter Seven

I will come and destroy Satan and his lost souls for good.
Satan knows what is coming, peoples that side with him,
which makes him stronger and fearless. He believes that he
can defeat God now because he has more strength by
having more followers.

Even Satan fears the one and only God. God placed Satan
onto earth to see if he would change. Satan lives from all
the hate and bitterness from the lost souls of earth.

I told Saint Michael that I will write about meeting you and
what we talked about and tell everyone in the world using
social media. If I can gather all followers of God, we all go
in our different directions and send the word of God over
the world by internet and by media.

There are believers who will help you because they believe
in God. They murdered Jesus and all his apostles over time.
This might happen to you as well, my son.

Remember, Jesus was followed by Satan, and he tried to
tempt him all the time.

Have no fear about dying in the name of God, for many
followers of God believe in him. Satan will try to stop them
as well; one might be working for Satan just like the one
who deceived Jesus.

Trust yourself from here on, tell everyone you meet our
story and see what happens.

They will know you are telling the truth. This world has changed, and not for the good, they all know this. Those who read the scriptures, know, and understand everything about God.

They will come to your aid and help you out. God's work must be done on this planet called earth.

This planet will be destroyed over time starting in 2020. Tell them all how the world will end in your story. Tell them the year and date this world will end for good.

The day Saint Michael returns to this planet, they will see the sun glow bright, and I will destroy Satan for good. For this is the will of God, and all lost souls still living will be sent to die with Satan, even those in the valley.

So, everyone better start repenting before this happens, this is the word from God himself. You will feel lonely, most of these kids in today's world do not believe in God.

The ultimate battle will be with Satan and his followers. I will ride in with force with my other Angels and in God name.

Time will no longer exist, after "Satan's Death." Your job is to save the weak and blinded humans who have lost all faith in God.

Even if they made mistakes by following Satan while on this earth, it's never too late to turn around and repent. No human was ever born perfect, each of their Gods they pray to, they know God will help them in their "Darkest Hour."

You will show no fear in serving God. You will be forgiven for what you did on this earth.

Go out and serve God even with all your pain, and remember when you asked me your question before "If this was Hell?" Yes, it is. It was set up by God to see if temptation from Satan could make good people bad.

Then God wondered how bad Satan could be. Then God watched and saw the many murders and wars, and he was not pleased.

I asked Saint Michael, what if nobody believes me? Michael smiled at me and said, God, sent his Son once to gather followers, and people followed because they believed in him, known as Jesus.

Then humans murdered him, God watched and waited and brought him back to life, for those who believers they seen the power of God. This was how we tried to save humanity. Then we took Jesus back to heaven, to sit and stay beside his Father.

Remember Judas, this one person who did this to the Son of God, he is in the valley awaiting his fate still to this day with many others.

Everyone will meet their fate who worked with Satan in bad ways and will await their final judgement from God. Time does not exist outside of this planet.

Many might end up in the "Valley of Death," which is a place every soul cannot move or talk.

It is a place for sinners just to look at each other as the new dead souls walk through this valley.

When Satan starts to feel his power weakening. He will come and find you with his Son the Anti-Christ. He will do everything in his power to try to convince you to stop.

He cannot hurt you in any way my son, so have no fear knowing God is with you.

Chapter Eight

Humans on this earth have stopped believing in any higher power or religions. They are acting like those before them, faith has stopped because the parents did not guide the greatest gift the Lord God could give them, which were children.

Humans use money and lust to hurt each other; they forgot that God gave them the gift of children. They failed as parents, even though you did he told me. You lost your faith and stopped believing in God, and you were given wonderful sons.

You never tried to tell them about God his Son Jesus. Why is this, he asked me? I fell to my knees before him, and I told him I lost all my faith. I started to believe in Fate instead, like it was meant to be.

Many things that I see in my dreams I've written inside my book as well. Yes, but why did you not choose Faith and speak about God and placed my name or even Satan's name within it.

People would have believed more in you, and you would have grown more by now. I told him I understood, and I wish I could take it all back and start over.

Then I looked up while I was still on my knees toward St. Michael and yelled out; I was mad at you and God, I felt abandoned and lost.

I was doing the work of evil, and my mind got lost. I did not believe you would come back to me, even after this power I had seeing humans fate of when and how they were going to die.

I saw so much in my mind and in my dreams, I would walk by people in stores and know what would happen to them. Death was my best friend; he was all I knew in my life.

Everyone I ever known has died. I got to the point that I never wanted to leave my home and just wanted to be alone.

He said yes, we took your friends from you, nobody can cheat death. I told my wife about meeting you before we got married. She believed me.

St. Michael said, every human on earth wished they could start over and not have sinned. Then asked me if I was still up to this task. Do you have the strength to act in the name of your Father? I said yes.

He then reached out his hand for me to take, I reached for his and he pulled me close to him and standing me up.

He placed his hand upon my forehead and yelled looking upward and shouted out; "Then you are forgiven for all your sins on this planet called Earth."

Go and start your new book and use the power that the Gods gave you, as a gift and write your novel and ask for help from all who believes in God.

Tell all the believers and non-believers, tell the rich and the poor, tell the strong and the weak, that God has had enough and he is not happy, then tell them I will be coming, tell them your month and day this will happen.

Believers will come; this I promise you. Go into churches and preach the word of God. Money will do them no good anymore, they will support you more than you think in all your travels.

Fear nothing and nobody, meet with leaders of churches, for you will stand beside each leader of these churches and help them repent in front of their followers.

You help people on this earth from here on, awaken the fools who stopped or never believed in the God.

Tell the world what is coming, and I will be the very first face they will see, when death comes down upon them from this worthless place called Hell.

There are many people in need of help, but the only help many poor souls will receive is after they die.

You tell these other leaders from other Countries, if they do not follow the word of God, they will be turned into dust.

Gods Angels know which souls to save, and who to bring before God for forgiveness. You must never fear death, he told me! Remember your visions from your dreams.

Would Satan and his demons find out when this world will end?

Saint Michael Stated to me: Satan and his followers will never believe in the truth.

No non-believer on earth will be able to hear the truth, speak the truth, or see the truth.

Those who will hear the truth will know; not to fear the word of God.

Those who can speak the truth; Will stand by your side.

Those to can see the truth; Will see that God is with them.

Those who try to deceive you; Knows the Truth, but will not be able to Speak of it, for they will be judged on their silence.

Chapter Nine

God has waited and learned how Satan worked overtime he used corruptions through humans. Children seem to fall into Satan tricks very easily. God now knows this is not going to change on this planet.

This is why the world will be no more, and Satan himself must die, along with all his many followers, the earth will remain dark for Satan followers until all of his lost souls is destroyed for the last time.

Those leaders of churches have paid staffers and teachers who are taught to manipulate others. This is the work of Satan, and they all know this. They all will read this book and see what they have become, some will change and most will not.

They will come to you and want to meet with you. They will try to get you to change your thoughts and help them mislead their followers. For they will not want to lose power or their money.

Some will even help you with your mission and work with you to help change the non-believers. Some of these people can be saved, tell them it is never too late to repent and change.

Not all prophets or preachers are bad people, and those good ones will be the ones who will help you with those non-believers.

They must tell all their followers; That God is real, God loves is true, God will see them after they die.

Never try to fool God, for God knows everything before it comes into their mind.

You must make sure they understand along with people in this world that you are speaking in the name of the Lord thy God. Humans cannot act like Gods walking on this earth, they can-not judge each other.

If other humans genuinely believe in God himself, they will stand by your side and preach the word of God for all to hear.

People can pray many times of the day, all day if they want too, because God hears all prays. It prays that gives God more strength and makes him happy. Many heads of Churches could have helped people in their lifetime, but they choose not to.

Most will love their money more than God. They are the ones who will never see the wrong they have done and convince themselves they are still sending the right message, but they do this only for wealth.

These are the ones that will die a horrific death, and their souls will never enter Heaven, their souls will be left in the valley of death by an Angel.

Their bodies will turn to ash along with their souls and Satan. Their followers will start to come over to your side. Because the truth of God has been challenged many times before, and God struck them all down before.

These false profits are nothing new to God, he has seen many of them. They always lose in the end, tell them all when you meet them. This is not a choice, it is a demand from God himself.

I will bring Satan to his knees to bow before God and Slay him dead and hand Satan soul into Gods hands. Once this happens a crack in the universe will open and there will be no more darkness anywhere.

All souls will be judged in Heaven, even those from the valley. For the will of God will be done.

There will be peace forever after, or until our father decides when and if the earth will ever be born once again. He might return humans back to life there, as he has done in the past.

Satan cannot corrupt anyone once his soul is turned into dust, and he will be no more. Right now, humans need wisdom.

They need Faith in their Heart and Love in their souls, and they need to read the scriptures and repent. Tell them to pray to the only God that hears all.

Tell them that God has sent you with a message, and you are speaking the words from God himself.

Remind them that God still loves them, and he will welcome those who have repented to his home in Heaven. Satan's power grew from the souls of all hate from humans.

God has had enough, and there will be a storm coming, and not for the good of humanity on this place called earth.

Tell the world that God has not forgotten them, and he loves all his children living here on earth.

Before I leave here for good, know that you are speaking in the name of "The Almighty," for I am just a servant of thy Father.

Know one last word I will speak to you about. Many people have read all the good books of their choice; in whatever religion they believe. But tell them there is only one Almighty, and they will stand before him and be judged.

Those with Faith, will be by your side, they will be overcome by your news from God. They will come far to hear what you have to say or watch and listen on a social network. You and your people will go to those who cannot come to you.

I then asked Saint Michael, "Who is the second beast to come?

You met him once in this life. For he is the Son of Satan, and he has gathered many followers for his Father, he has fooled many people because of his wealth and kindness.

He can jump from one powerful body to another; he is the most dangerous demon of all because he loves war and has billions of dollars.

Satan has demons or you might call them apostles.

He has built a great empire here on earth. He feels he himself can take on God once again with the power he obtained from all the sinners on this earth. This Son of Satan is the Anti-Christ.

He is extraordinarily rich and powerful, and his followers will work in ways to defeat you. We will help guide and wake up those who have forgotten our father.

We will still be watching from the Heavens over you. You have been the one chosen to tell the world what is coming.

Because Satan believes, he has you in your grasp by the evil you have done here on earth for him. Satan is an Angel who lives from lies and grows strong from the actions of others who do not believe in God and only think about making money, killing, and controlling others in any way they can.

The more money they make, the more powerful these people become. They all meet at times and grow stronger as humans, but Satan laughs at them, and help guides these Atheist's to greater powers.

Chapter Ten

Satan controls them like puppets on a string. They have more material things than any human can have and still wants more just to have it.

These rich humans know they have fallen into Satan will, and still, they go to church or flood churches with money. They know they can buy anything on this planet.

They feel they can buy their way into Heaven, then we even have priests, preachers and government officials taking their money and selling their souls to Satan himself.

Some do terrible things with it. Preachers, Reverends, Pastors, Evangelist, Priest all different names from all different faiths.

Many of them lie and obtain many followers by using the name of God. I know there are many diverse types of religions. God is the Father of all different religions and has many names from these diverse groups.

This saddens God very much. These leaders had all these followers feeding them money and they kept it all for themselves and their families. It wrong and they will pay the price when they meet God.

They all will be brought before God and judge as False Profits, just like in the past.

They walk around like Gods, with bodyguards and feel like nobody can touch them, but they themselves have lost faith in God over having wealth.

St. Michael said to me. What would you do if you became rich and had great wealth? I told him I would help others out who needed it. Money was never important to me, and I grew up poor. I would have taken care of the poor and those in need.

I would never watch others suffer around this world if I had the money some of these people have. I took a trip to another country and seen how poor they were and tried to understand how their country worked. I believe you; he said to me.

Nothing is free in this world I said, he agreed with me because he understood how this world works.

Jesus had little to work with, yet he travel the world and many followed him. It is all different now.

God's followers will take exceptionally loving care to help you on your quest, and you all God's followers will help those in need, and you and those believers will get this done one way of another.

Satan and his son the Anti-Christ will have no more power. Other evil demons will vanish from a slow death, and their souls with never again waken.

The day before you die my son. You will face both Satan and his son by yourself. Satan and his son the Anti-Christ. They will feel a power within your body and soul.

You will know the one thing they will want to know. They will want to know when and how this earth will end, but you will never tell them. They will believe they won and cause many problems upon humans and earth within one full day of time.

But remember they never heard what you told your followers, and your followers can never speak when asked by these two. So do not ever fear either of them, show no weakness, for you know the truth, and I will come for you as you leave this place called Hell.

Even as you write this in your book, they will never see it, because each book which is read will have the words from God.

For I will leave you now Michael, and you can tell everyone in this world, good or bad, what is coming their way. Some will laugh, many will follow, for the true believers of God will defend you with their life's.

They will help get the word out that God is still strong and for all to start repenting before this world end.

God has already forgiven you from all your sins you ever did on this earth for Satan. This living Hell will die out very quickly when I ride in and destroy everything in my path.

Go out and tell everyone, and have Faith, and never have any more doubts about what you are doing because you are working in the name of the Father, his Son, and the Holy Ghost.

Do you remember any prayer's Michael? A couple I stated.

Say a prayer to God he is listening right now.

I then dropped to my knees again and held my head high and said: Our Father, who art in heaven, hallowed be thy Name, thy kingdom come, thy will be done, on earth as it is in heaven.

Give us this day our daily bread. And forgive us our trespasses, as we forgive those who trespass against us. And lead us not into temptation but deliver us from evil.

Saint Michael told me - God is smiling right now, you made him happy. You did well. Pray when you feel lonely or you need strength, for we will be beside you from here on. Pray with others or teach others to pray with you.

You will have this power come over you like no other. Satan or his son could never say the prayer like you just did.

They do not even like to hear those words. Fire would spit out of their mouths if they heard you say that prayer. Use it as a weapon and nothing will ever stop you.

And remember the last thing I told you before you die. Satan and his son will be their trying to get into your mind and soul. They will be confused.

Just pray with those words in your mind, and they will turn away and run with fire falling from those words.

Go in peace Michael, and now you know how Satan works. Start new and travel and teach the word of God in this world once again, for all of Gods people need it so bad.

Time is running out for this world, you now know this, and you know when this earth will falter. I will see you soon, go in our father's name, and fear nothing. For God is with you

Chapter Eleven

That was the last time I spoke to Saint Michael the Arch Ange in 2020. He came back even when I had cursed him and God. It took me many years in my life to know there is a real God, I sat on my knees for hours, but I felt Stronger.

I will tell you what needs to be taken to help weaken Satan. Stop Hating each other, Stop Killing each other, If you know it's wrong or feel it's wrong, then don't do it!

I will tell everyone what needs to be done and together let us do the work of God.

Start believing in God, start helping people in need, start speaking about God to others, start showing the gift of kindness to those who need it.

The end will be coming and everyone on this planet will die. I will put the date of the end of this world in this novel.

If you believe in God and would like to join me, the cost of me teaching you God's work is free. I will only ask everyone who reads this novel to spread the word of God and help other understand how God really works. I can be contacted at michaelmckay712@yahoo.com

I want nothing from nobody; all I want before I die is to help teach you to believe in God. If you can't give God time out of your life, then I really can't help you out, and I have to tell you, there is no help for you ever.

You must give up your soul to your higher power, or to whomever you pray to. God hears everything from everybody.

Your prayers gives God strength and beliefs that many humans can be saved. God spoke to me through Saint Michael and wanted me to get everyone a message; He Love you all and It is not too late to ask for forgiveness.

This world, as you know it, will be ending, this is a fact! I know people's fears but here is the bottom line. You live and you die, it's what you do while living those counts.

There is nothing to fear in life or death if you believe in God. Sometimes people has to find God themselves in their own ways.

As soon as those lost souls find God, things will change for them. Again, I have no idea why I was picked. I was not any big religious person ever in my life. I have read the Bible a couple of times in my life and have found God through others.

I was never a nice person on this planet, but I have been forgiven for my past and I believe nobody on the planet can judge me. I did good things within my life, but I felt the bad did outweigh the good.

God showed me he was real by looking out for me in life. I truly believe in God and in Heaven, I also know all too well about Satan.

I see the different between; "God and Satan," this is "Good vs. Bad." This is all a test to see if humans were strong enough to know the difference between the both.

We all get tested every day from both God and Satan.

Satan knew that he could corrupt me at any time he wished.

This was Satan way only to get me to understand he had my soul whenever he wanted to take it. By me cursing at God Almighty himself. This was Gods way to fool Satan. I am here telling everyone about what happen in my life with God.

A Brother from the Dominican Friars from the Province of Saint Martin de Porres. Brother Art Kirwin, whom I knew from many years ago, came to visit me and my wife at that time.

It was more than thirty years ago. I found it strange that he would show up out of nowhere and give me a Bible. He told me to always keep this near you.

He told me; He knew what happened between me and God, and God sent him to me and for him to deliver this Bible to me. Then I thought to myself, how did Brother Art ever know what happened?

I found this to be very strange because I never told anyone about meeting Saint Michael and Brother Art was another human.

He never gave up on me when he knew me growing up in life, he tried many times to show me Gods will, and I never gave into him.

He gave me a Bible more than thirty-year ago in 1990. It was new and in the box. I kept it beside my bedroom drawer all this time. I never picked it up or even read it.

Months ago, I opened it and felt something come over me, as I read the first few lines, tears fell from my eyes. I know my friend Brother Art was an Angel sent from the high Heavens.

After I finish reading this one Bible, I turned and seen this glow once again in my room and St. Michael was before me once again. He came back to me once I was done with the last page.

He asked me if I enjoyed the new Bible. I smiled and told him I did, and I asked him about Father Art. Yes, St. Michael said to me, he is a good Angel, and he was sent to you as a test by me, my son.

You were in your darkest hours and sending you this Bible through Brother Art lit up your soul, and I knew I would visit you once again after you read it. You will meet him again. He loves you and your wife; he gave me a Saint Joseph Edition - The New American Bible.

After this book I am writing, I am going to read it again. There is a message in it for me from him.

I will carry and read this until I hear from all the people who want to help spread the word of God with me.

We will carry the word of God to every Country in the world and read what I have been told to tell everyone.

Our Father is kind and forgiving, he created man and women in hopes all will be faithful to him. Love, strength, kindness, and those who believe in him, make God stronger to protect those in need, and bring them back to heaven to their loved ones.

I was also told from Saint Michael that God felt that people on this one planet have let him down more than from other planets. God has thought the many wars, senseless murders, and genocides that has happened in this world was the work of Satan.

God realized people had their own choices whether to conduct these evil deeds from powerful people. It is called; "Free Will" God will give you the rope you need to hang yourselves. God feels a weakness from people on earth, and with what is happening on this planet.

Money is the root of all evil, without a doubt. Everyone knows this. God made life quite easy for everyone to live. To grow families, to love each other. To pray every day to him, and to thank him for his kindness.

To learn and educate each other, and to believe in God through each other. But Satan, produced money and gold.

He knew who to give it to so he could use his powers over them. If they only knew about Satan and remembered that God and his Son Jesus loves all who believe in them.

Each human knows not to Sin, but if you do, pray and repent. God gave us quite simple rules to live by, and we could not even do this for him.

Humans have messed up everything ten times over. God never gave up and kept trying.

God is the meaning of life and love.

Saint Michael asked me why it was so hard for humans to follow these simple rules. Humans make everything harder in life by wanting money and power, then to act like Gods and control everything and everyone the way they want them to be.

This has happened from way back in the days when men's road on horsebacks and killed people over religions they believed in.

God overlooked this belief at first, then he saw how wars started over what others prayed to and what others believed in. Then they killed each other for not believing in their God. What don't people understand?

Even this made God hold his head down, and he asked himself why? Wars were fought over what one other believes in. God could never understand this either, God gave your life which is very precious

Chapter Twelve

Those who never believed in God. They could have found their path, they knew right from wrong, they knew good from bad, they knew how to help one another or to hurt one another, it was all about having power!

They all knew this before they acted in such a manner, as it was the right thing to do.

They all let their anger get the best of them. God put this moment of hesitation in everyone's mind before they were born upon this earth. They had that one second of thought whether it is right or wrong. These choices are made by each human by themselves.

Satan is out their tempting each person every second of the day. But they still had that one choice, to carry it out or not.

They could have stayed with their beliefs in God and stayed true to God. But no, they worked with Satan and forgot about God. They all took the bite from that one apple!

God set rules for people to live by on this planet. Nobody ever has gotten it right ever since he first made man and women.

I want this to sink into your heads. I am not here to write a new Bible for you. This is a message from the big guy himself.

He knows I am going to tell you in simple terms. I going to tell everyone that God feels most younger people have lost their faith in him, and I believe he is right.

He wants these younger people to understand that he is there for you, and when you are ready to start to believe in God, then you must repent all your sins and change your ways in life.

It does not go unnoticed, that most older people always comes over to God knowing they will be dying soon. He will ask them what they did in their lives to help other people, and did you teach them about God.

Just because you go to church and pay the church will never buy you a seat in Heaven. It does not work that way. You take care of those while you are alive, then you will feel better as you die.

Older people should spread the word of God to these younger people, many of them never found God in their lifetime.

Kids in today's world do not believe in anything. If they only stopped playing video games, they would learn about God.

They will have different avenues to decide on which paths they wish to take. They will find love and happiness up one road, and Satan in the other.

They can always say no to Satan and turn and take the other path in the road towards God.

They would act differently and respect older people, because elders know more than they will never know. Then when they get older, they will follow by intuition.

Knowledge is power. God gave everyone a brain, most use it to be stupid, or to cause chaos in this world. Technology is destroying our world and things will not get any better.

I was told how they received this technology which was never meant to happen on this planet. I can't tell you why or how humans came up with this new technology, because it would take away from what you need to know about God.

They have stumbled across this technology, and over the years, they found how to use it only to destroy each other. From fighting in wars, or to take over other countries. I know how they received this knowledge, and nobody has the right to control another human.

Nobody should judge each other from earth for this is Gods job when one dies.

It sad and shameful that we made God sad. Because we all are acting out in ways that were never meant to be. We look at our leaders in churches and our political world and praised them instead of God himself.

All these leaders are all just humans, and our leaders cannot lead the right way, but many of us still follow these leaders. Why is this? Why can't we follow God this way.

This goes for all religious leaders as well, from the Pope to every one of these leaders of God.

Some religious speakers bring false words from the Bible just for money they take in. "Free Speech" and "Free Will" are totally different!

Don't be giving all these phony leaders money each morning on TV or every week either in any church telling you that you need to "Sow a Seed" Pray as a group, pray together over a meal and be thankful for the food you eat every day.

Pray while you are walking, singing, walking your dogs or in your homes. Talk about God every day and many times a day to others. Teach your young ones about God and how great he is.

Worship God and thank him for bringing his Son onto this earth and to die for every one of us. For this happened and this very true. You all are starting to see changes in these weather patterns that have already started to change.

This is one of the first steps to happen by God. Each day of every year the weather will get worse. You are going to see more flooding with holes opening beneath the ground.

Stronger Hurricanes with categories seven and eight take out many cities and states. Tornadoes will grow over category five and grow into eight or nine. These will be the starts of removing and cleaning out the evil on this earth.

You are going to see Cities and States starts to fall apart from the weather and stronger earthquakes.

The best will come when more Tsunami hits land around the world, volcanoes will erupt, one of the top five will be Yellowstone.

You will see the United States crack between states. Cities will tumble into the oceans as many have before. God believes if people do not get on track, your souls will parish along with this world we live in. This will be the start of humanity suffering and ending.

It does not matter how you die; it matters when you die, with what you did in your life and then stand before God. Then you will be judged, and it will be too late for you to say you're sorry!

These will all be signs of God sending everybody a message throughout this world. The world will be ending. Yes, I know when, and I also know when I will die.

God smiles and watches as humans try to find other planets to live on, and what humans are trying to do in space. Let me tell everybody one thing I know to be a fact. We have never been into deep space. Ever!

We can only get to the earth's atmosphere. This is where all those satellites up there and are track and watch over everything on the ground.

God said man would never understand the universe. For that is where all the answers are, and man is to blind to see this. God does love a few thing people have done on this earth.

He loves music and the writing of songs. He loves poems people write.

He loves seeing how smart people have gotten. He looks down and he sees everyone happy when gifted people play their music.

God love music, sometimes Angels hear God singing these songs in Heaven. It makes him happy from the words or just the music itself, Saint Michael told me.

God has sent sprits down to earth before and watched people fall to their knees when true believers come forth.

There is more hate toward God than ever before. He has been angered before and destroyed this world many times because of Satan and his demons having this power to manipulate humans.

This is when all the worlds will open, and God will give humans one more chance, without any evil in it, in a wonderful place in the universe. They will live like the other worlds in the universe.

But again, I will tell you once Satan is dead, and if you are lucky ones to go to another place with new people on it. At night you will never see darkness nor the stars.

You will see other planets and meet other people who believe in God from those planets.

People do visit this place called earth, either by "Time or by Flight." People have advanced far better than the people here on earth. People from earth are looking in space.

They will never find anything. All the answers humans
need to know are in the oceans of earth.

The oceans have destroyed earth many times before. You
can find many cities under that water. This is where Satan
lives.

The waters and storms that come to any lands have washed
away many people and cities since the beginning of time.

The oceans are wonderful, if you ever sat on a beach and
looked over the ocean, you would find peace within your
heart.

Man can never fight the waves of the oceans. God has
given you all the food you can eat from the many oceans.
Yet, you all have found ways to destroy these great oceans
by polluting them.

People on earth have contaminated the air and water,
humans need to breathe fresh air for their lungs and drink
water to live. But yet, it's all being destroyed by other
humans for their love of money. Why is this?

Chapter Thirteen

I want to tell everyone right now because everyone loves to read books still. The number one book on this earth ever sold is "The Bible." This is a fact.

People are confused about the Bible. Jesus never wrote it himself; followers of Jesus wrote it, great authors of that time.

They could never put everything in one book. But it was written to help guild humans and help them find their path in life. God wanted people to be happy, make families, and love each other.

He knew he placed Satan amongst everyone on this planet. He had to know if people would give themselves to Satan or stay with the God that created humanity. Somehow people have twisted the words around in the good book called the Bible.

Humans could have worked together and been as one. Instead, humans fought for land, claimed their own Countries, and challenged each other and competing with each thinking one was better than the other. This is not what or why God created humans.

He gave each one of us a chance to live a good and happy life, then he would take you back into the Heavens and you would live once again with your families. Or be placed on another place to start over.

All those sperm cells from man fed into women, one cell gave you a child to cherish and teach as they grew older and taught to be kind and follow in Gods footsteps.

But still, somewhere in their life. They fall from grace and take the wrong paths in life, or the parents never did their jobs, or kids having babies' way too young in their life. This is all wrong.

This was not Gods way from making humans. He watches the drug's use and the spread of a virus to one another. God had punished people before with the Black Death and much more. God works in mysterious ways is true.

The important thing about the Bible. It was meant for humans to understand and follow the meaning of life itself. It explains to everyone about life and tells everyone about death. There are good and bad statements written in this one book or all good books humans believe in.

Most people misinterpret each paragraph, and I can understand why this happens. Of each person in this world 65% read their informative book often. It helps calm their souls and most believe it will help them get into Heaven once they die.

This is only true if they talk about what they read and share their knowledge with others to teach the word of God for free, and if they followed the good books, in all religions.

Yes, it will get them into heaven, only if it is not misused to make their followers Blasphemy or use their flocks to use and abused them for wealth.

Before Saint Michael came back to me. I wanted everyone to understand why you are living and start spreading the word of the God.

God is not asking much from humans. He would like everyone in this world to work together as one and repent together. It is not that hard to do when you think about it. For those who stand in our way and refuse to hear the word of God, they will become lost.

All these Dictators in this world who are leaders of many of these Countries and hold their people to only believe in them, will Falter. Once this happens, things will become worse in those countries from their new leaders.

For they will start a mighty war against the world. I see Russia fighting a new war. Not working with the United States along with Israel and England, India will have a choice to make.

They will have to decide what is best for their country.

These countries want to rule the world. Countries like China and North Korea, the Middle East and even Russia. Iran and other countries from the Middle East will all join the Middle East and will come with all forces to attack Israel first.

They believe this will get America to save Israel from doom. This new virus was just a test by China. But what China gave to this world, it will go away for a brief time but then return and kill many more humans.

That is when China will release more germ warfare upon this planet. They have been working on some of the deadliest known diseases to humanity for years.

These viruses will bring death to many people. This is why Russia will have to help fight against China and North Korea. These overpopulated countries will need room for their people.

These are all Dictators we will have to try and deal with, and you cannot deal with these people. This is a fact!

North Korea, and China will attack America, you can count on this happening. They want to repopulate, and they have the people to do what they want and have the power to do what they wish . . . China believes in their own History.

They will never accept defeat from any other nation. They hate America without a doubt; we will hear a great roar of thunder from the skies above. I will explain and tell you more when we start speaking with each other. I need to meet with other followers on how we should continue with getting the word out.

This job will get done because its Gods will. I stated before in this books that I would never fear death, now you know why.

You will find out that one day the world will end.

Those that have money has to remember that you cannot take it with you. It is good to take care of your family but understand they must do good with what you left them

Chapter Fourteen

I believe people will gather by bringing God back into people's hearts. They will feel Rejuvenated; We must awaken them by the words of God.

Whoever reads this book I would hope you will start teaching your young ones the word of God, and when people start waking up and thanking God each and every day, then it would make this world a better place.

Well, the time has come to help God defeat Satan, now is your time to help God out. You will be challenged by those phony profits because their money flow will slow down. You all must realize you cannot take your money with you when you die.

I would never play using the name of God for the sake of money. If I had the money these other religion people have. I would have had peace in this world ten times over.

These Phony Preachers, Bible Thumpers and Evangelist and Priest. You got these big millionaires and billionaires doing nothing for the poor people. I cannot believe some people have billions of dollars.

You tell me they cannot go into other countries and fix their problems with some of their money. This makes me sick.

I would have gone into these small poor countries and built Hospitals, Schools, taught them how to grow food, get them free running water.

Give them a government to be proud of and build real houses for them to live in instead of a little hut.

Angels visits this planet all the time, and I'm sure many others have spoken to other Angels.

I know many people have had that feeling that you have done this before, like walking down the street, or driving in a car. Well, you have done this before, many of you have lived other lives before here on earth.

I was an extremely poor kid growing up. It is just so sad to see people with great wealth, not help everyone they can.

What do they think they are going to buy their way into Heaven? Shame on all the extraordinarily rich people.

I can see leaving some money for your kids and family members, but they should leave a legacy behind before they die, that would be epic.

Chapter Fifteen

Nobody could spend One Billion dollars in a lifetime. A person with one billion dollars could spend $100,000 dollars a day for 27 years and still have money left over.

Now tell me why or how a person has tens of billions of dollars, and can't help humanity?

I hope this wakes most of you people up!

I am incredibly sad right now writing this to everyone. I just do not understand why the wealthy don't stand up and do the right thing for other humans.

We cannot judge any human on this planet, yet we all do it all the time. This is wrong, no human can judge another. This is the word of God.

This is what our United Nations should be doing. But they all just sit around this big table, talk every day, and live a good life, and they do nothing at all.

Nobody cannot force people to believe in God. I'm not asking anyone for money at all, I'm selling this book at the lowest price the book company will allow me, and I'm not making any money from this novel. This should stand for something.

Poor people learn to live because they are strong-willed people. Please believe in God. There is so much more I must tell people of faith.

To those believers in God, you must have faith and trust. For those who do not, will pay with your souls when you die.

When that time comes you will be begging and pleading in front of God for one more chance. he will tell you all that you had your last warning.

Come on people you never thought this day was going to come. God has had enough!

All these false preachers; They have been doing the same thing for many long years. They are no better than politicians in Washington. Stay there, do nothing, collect money, and keep it.

It is like these preachers buying their own Jets for fifty two million dollars to fly around to the many homes they own. God knows what these false prophets are doing. They will be judged when they meet him, and he will deal with them.

I will spread the word of God and tell people what must be done for free. If there is any hate in my journey, it will come from Satan and his followers.

Because I will serve our father. "We will not just be knocking on doors. We will be kicking the door in to awaken people. Just to get our point across to all these people who has forgotten about "God" .

God will smile, and he will thank you for bringing back these younger kids and those who forgotten him on this earth.

You all must repent to God before this happens. He can destroy this world anytime he wishes, I know God really want to see if these nonbelievers can get on their knees and start believing in him once again.

Drop to your knees just read this line in this book, and asked God for forgiveness, and then tell him you love him, and you will go out and spread the word of God to others. When you get out of bed each morning, thank God.

God does not care what color you are or where you are from. Biologically and genetically, we are the only humans on this planet.

People believed in God before and people must believe in God again; it does not matter to whom you pray. There is only one Higher Power, and he loves you all, and all he is asking is peace within this planet, or pay with what will happen with your souls?

Everyone would be happy if they dismantle all weapons, help each other, stop all wars, and hate on this planet. Work and help each other out.

This is very possible to do, money and power has destroyed this world and started wars for many years along with oil and gold. This is all stuff which comes out of the earth for free. Why must people fight and killed each other for it.

You asked about work and health insurance, people are dying over these greedy companies. You help your older people out for free.

You help farmers with their crops; you work and help each other out by using your minds and bodies. You work for four days and be with your family the rest of the time.

Technology will destroy everything in life I once wrote in a book. There are needs and wants. If you need it, buy it. If you want it, then you do not need it. It is remarkably simple. Everything on this planet you can get for free, you need food, then grow it.

Each city and town can help each other out. Everyone will be equal; you do not need any Government to tell you what and how you should live. This is why Jesus came on to this earth. God works for free.

And this should tell you something about money and humans.

Chapter Sixteen

When Jesus walked on this earth, he taught people how to grow food from the ground and shared it with all that needed it. They also had plenty of fish from the oceans around them. Even though money was around back in those days. Jesus taught people how to live without it.

For he knew what would become of money in the future. Money is the root of all evil. We all know this, people will kill just to have it. Ask yourselves why?

Satan knows this as well. For his son, the Anti - Christ is one of the riches' men in the world. And he has people eating out of his hands, because those with the most money are the ones who have the power, and they have the most followers.

Even those who follow some of these leaders of faiths, they all became extraordinarily rich people. Saint Michael and I even talked about how people look up to all these movie actors and singers.

I told him I have met many entertainers and so-called famous people. I never thought much of them.

He asked me why I was different than other people who placed them all on a pedestal. I told him they were just people with talent.

I told him about people who play on the streets for free and they leave a case open for people to place money in there if they wish to. These street performers really do it for free.

They sound just as good. I told him there was a lot of wasted talent in this world. I told him I traveled to England and many people are homeless and living on the streets or they perform in hopes people will give them money.

For those who believe God is happy with you for believing in him and never giving up with what he expects from everybody on this earth.

I remember everything tis Angle told me. Have no fear from anything or anybody, for we are away's by your side. There is nothing more for me to tell you, for you know what must be done were the last words spoken.

That was the last time I saw and spoken to Saint Michael.

I am sure people will have many questions. I know I cannot answer every question in one day. I will set up different days and times which will be convenient for everyone.

You will understand that I will need to heal, we can even speak on the phone or text.

I wish to make God happy by bringing humans back into his life and bring God back into their life's. If you are not a believer in God or any higher power, this is your choice, and I will respect your wishes, and that's all I will say on this matter.

I have met many people who do not believe in God, and they have tried at times to get back into good graces with God, and this is okay, because I believe just by these people recognizing there is a God is a step in the right direction.

The only person you need to follow is the God you pray to.
There is nothing to fight about, this is only one God who
has many names, and he hears all who repent and pray to
him.

He will forgive those who repent before this world is
destroyed. Yes, you will have to confess to him and tell
him why and how you acted out with others on this planet
earth. Tell him the truth. You can-not get over on God, so,
please do not try, remember that God Loves you.

This message is especially important for all to understand.

What wisdom God has, what patience, what love for us he
still holds onto, God is forgiving. It is giving me chills just
knowing he loves us after all the terrible things we all have
done on this planet. God knows Satan has grown with
power on this earth.

God knows and understand how Satan obtained this power;
it was through the weakness through all humans. By
following Satan and doing whatever he wanted through
temptation. Everyone must save themselves and their
families when danger is coming your way by all and any
means.

Terrible things are going to happen; they have already
started.

Yes, Human will suffer and hurt. But as you dying, say the
lords pray and an Angel will lead you to God as you walk
through the valley, then all your pain will go away
extremely fast.

All this madness, which is going on in this world right now, it seems to me that Satan is doing his greatest work. So, let us just hope for the best.

Satan is at work wanting to replace curtain leaders of different countries. There will be another great war on this planet, and it will be soon.

We will be attacked by other countries within the next twenty years. Many dictators hate our country, and they never forgot what we did in our past to other countries in wars. They will show us no mercy, but in the end, America will show them none either, and America will destroy them and win after many deaths on both sides.

There are other forces living on this planet who are trying very hard to stop this from happening, but they can't even stop the inevitable.

This is why God has had enough. After this war on America, many people will suffer for many years before God sends in his Angles to finish the job.

This will be the end of the world as we all know it, no more life on this planet, and everything will become silent.

There is nothing to speak about, all will answer to God when everything ends. It will happen for all to see the real anger within God himself.

Chapter Seventeen

Many times, we have watched leaders try to lead and failed because they were not meant to be leaders, They just wanted the power, this has happen a few times here in America and other countries.

This world is changing, and evil is starting to form within people's minds. They seem to be fighting on what side to take. People on the earth have stopped believing in God, but the great coming of God is ready to unleashed his powers amongst those who are here living here in hell.

People living in this hellish place has never seen or ever understood the change's which has been happening on this planet they call earth.

We are all responsible for destroying this planet we live on. We are all guilty for the oceans being polluted, lands being poison which effect peoples bodies. Yes, it is real, yes, it is happening, and It is very sad.

We allowed this all to happen over the many years to our own planet from companies growing and making bigger money from humans. When these companies get caught, they pay a small fine and it all goes away, and then they start all over again.

Humans never thought about God being everywhere, he has been watching how humans act. Time has run out for those who have used Gods name over money and greed.

I have carried this curse with me for many years now. Saint Michael told me it would be a gift. I see it differently than a gift, it was no gift watching everyone you loved or known die around you.

When everybody I've known started dying around me, my last friend who died I had known him for 47 years of my life. I became very lonely, and I stayed to myself. I'm still by myself to this day, I don't want to know new people or have close friend only because I will know their fate of being a friend.

I speak to God every day and I block out all sounds and just use my brain.

I feared meeting new people because of this gift. I have met death, and we now have become good friends.

I have been in hospitals to see people and I held their hands and just told them to let go and everything would be all right, and they did and died later that night. People try so hard to keep living on this earth and It's hard for them to give up their lives, they refuse to let go and die as they suffer to live.

Dying is not a bad thing like I stated, it's the doorway to meet your maker. Remember this; Dying is not painful; You never die, please remember this.

What I mean by this is very simple, even if your soul is not welcome in Heaven, then your soul will enter; "The Valley of Death" and it will stay there for eternally.

You will meet your maker, and if you have done well for yourself on this planet, then you will be rewarded from God. Then you will meet your loved ones on the other side and be placed in another world forever with your loved ones.

Your souls never die if you please God and pray and repent to him. God is real, Heaven is real, and The Valley of Death is real.

God tries to send people messages all the time. But most times people are just so blind to see the messages he is sending you.

Death should only be feared by those who do not believe in God, or who break all the rules he had set for everyone. God knew his Son Jesus would be murdered by humans.

There is no room for your soul in heaven with the hate you carry around with you.

When Jesus walked on the planet, he was a teacher, he walked the path of righteous, he helped out sick people, poor people, feed people by himself. He set the standard for everyone to walk in his footsteps, to do what he did, and love everyone you meet.

But it did not work out that way. People started taking Gods names in vain, stealing, killing, hating, bringing false idols before God, and there are many more.

All our father wanted from us was for all of us to believe in him and follow all his rules.

He knew many if not all, would fall into the temptations from Satan. This was God's way of testing humans. He wanted to welcome all those who believe in his Son Jesus in Heaven.

Look where we are in today's world, we are so divided, and people has lost their faith…

Those who came before God and repented and proved their love to him, God has shown mercy to many. He understands humans and loves us all "Unconditional."

It is funny when humans break every law they made for themselves, then, ends up in their prisons systems they created.

Yet they cannot follow one commandment from God which he made and gave you a life.

He has always felt a weakness from humans because he knows how we act and think. He knows and sees how fast humans turn and works with Satan.

I feel for bad for God because he carries us all on his shoulders. For him to forgive people from earth after how many of us all have deceived him.

Yet, we can stand before him, and he has the power to show compassion and love towards us. Then forgive us for all our sins from what we did here on earth.

If you ever looked at yourself in the mirror or at another human being.

God created people perfect. From our brains in our heads, right down to every body part, we are all walking computers, and all humans have one brain which is 80 percent waters. This is why humans need hydrate; we need to keep a balance for brain function.

Some people believe that alien from other planets created humans, and we are all their specimens. Okay if they really believe this, then who created the universe and those aliens? End of story!

Why do humans want to hurt someone they "Hate." Because it means they are following Satan temptations by using the word "Hate."

Now ask yourself why you should forgive people you Hate? Because now your following Gods will by "Forgiving" and show "Love and Compassion."

Yet God, will forgive you and everyone else if they pray to him and just ask him for forgiveness. This is called pure "Love."

God is only Love and he cares for all of us in this world. He asked very little of us. Yet, everyone who goes to church each week, then once they leave, they do not show that love they had in church towards each other.

Some people just go to church, to get it out of the way.

I have killed, lied, cheated, hated, and sinned just like any other human on this planet. I've never been perfect, but yet, here I am talking about God to all strangers.

There are many people like me on this earth, and I just told everyone some of the things I've done in my past, because it does not matter. I've have become a better person from my past experiences.

Humans need to stop thinking about the past, it's something you can't change. What you can change is the future, by looking at everything differently and not making your past mistakes. Yes, it's that simple!

One thing I've learned about friends from the past; Many of your Friends want you to do well in life, but they don't want you to do better than them. This is a fact!

Having Satan as a friend is the easiest thing to do. Fighting against him is the hardest thing to do. Because Satan and his son has always tempted humans. They never make you do anything, They just tempted you, and you chose to do it, just to get ahead in life. You think nobody in the high Heavens will ever notice.

It was your choice whether or not to do something bad from temptation from these two evil demons. Satan does not have the power to make anyone do anything, he has the power to used temptation, this is his greatest gift. People fall for it every time.

Those who take it and sin, Satan becomes more powerful in our world. Satan tempted Jesus many times. Do you believe Jesus ever had doubts about his Father the Lord God himself. No, he never even thought about Satan's temptations.

Where would we be right now if Jesus took Satan side? Jesus was much smarter than that. He knew temptation was wrong, he served his Father by believing in him and with him. Jesus made his choice once he was born.

Satan knew he could never defeat Jesus after that and stopped trying. Jesus became more powerful because he had more followers who believed he was the Son of God.

Could you imagine if Jesus has social media back in those days.

Jesus did an excellent job back in those days. Yes, he did use his powers to perform a few miracles, just to show the people from those day, it was from the power of God.

Chapter Eighteen

Satan was behind murdering Jesus, and he became very weak when Jesus came back to life once again. Jesus shows the world the power of his Father by dying and returning.

God has watch Satan very closely over time. To date, Satan has much of his power back on this planet, and each day he is growing stronger. He would like to take over the universe and then the high Heavens. Satan hates God, I believe he just wanted what God had, and he could not achieve his goals.

Remember what I wrote in my last chapter about (Many of your Friends want you to do well in life, but they don't want you to do better than them.)

This is what I believe what happened in Heaven when Satan wanted to Kill God and take over Heaven.

Everybody know about the great "Holy War" and believe it will be The Middle East against Israel. Wrong!

The Holy War will be between Satan and God, and this is why God is giving everyone one last chance to repent. Many people will die together, and, on that day, it will be the war of all wars!

This is why the great war will take place on earth, and it will be coming soon.

When I just told you Satan is stronger than ever before, He really is, because he feeds of humans sins, which gives him strength.

Saint Michael will come riding in with his army and take all the souls of those who worked for Satan first, this will take away some of Satan's power.

Then he will take his sons soul and then he will rip the soul from Satan and bring all those lost souls before God, and he will crush Satan and his son souls to dust, and all Satan's followers souls will turn to dust right on the spot…

For Satan will be no more.

People try to fool God all the time by pretending to love him and pray to him in front of others. This is so wrong.

Talk to God and tell him how you are feeling today. Tell him how your week was, tell him even though you are down, and nothing is working your way, you still believe in him, and asked him to help you, and to guide you in the right direction.

Everyone can do this from their own homes or out in the open sitting on a bench feeding birds. He hears everything and knows everything.

God sends many Angels down to this earth and have followed people to help guide humans on that right path. I know this as a fact.

Everything happens for a reason with humans. We hate, we kill, we start wars, we have much evil in us all. This is very true.

God knows this, and yes, it sadden God, but he knows, that when he created humans, and gave them free will, he knew Satan would act and try to change everything God created.

Even God knew placing humans here with Satan was a bad idea, but yet, it would be a great test for him to see how humans would act over the many temptations put before them.

God knew by Satan tempting everyone here on earth and balancing the scales between Good vs Evil, he wanted to see how many souls Satan could gather.

Humans held their own destiny in their hands, and all of us have failed at the highest levels. We have all let God down.

God never wanted to kill Satan, but now he knows he must, he is way too powerful. This is the reason God will destroy this planet with everyone on it.

Satan must be destroyed and that will be the will of God. Many people on earth right now are talking about Christianity being under attack, well it is. All who believe in God are under attack, this is why the start of 2020 was a very important date!

There is statue figure showing Saint Michael standing on top of Satan with a sword in hand.

Do you know why this statue was created? This was made in the 17th century by Peter Anton Von Verschaffelt.

Saint Michael is a warrior, make no mistake about this. He stands for all the good and he fights against all evil. Back in those days, an Angle was sent by God to visit earth and requested this statue be made for the future of mankind, and it was.

This was a statue made by man, because God wanted everyone to see the future and the past by looking at this statue.

God created the Black Plague in the 17th century, and it killed well over fifty million people. God wanted people of the future to look back at what happened from the Black Plague and why this statue was created.

It was to remind humans of what God did by sending the Plague to punish humans who followed Satan, and it was to remind humans of what will be if people continue to follow Satan.

So here we are in the year of 2025 in the 25th century and this statue still remains and still is standing tall in Rome, Italy. This is what will happen the day Saint Michael will return here to earth. He will fight Satan in the name of God and rip his soul out and bring his to God.

Satan doing his finest work right now here on earth, and many people here on earth who follow him are just making him stronger. I believe in Saint Michael and all the Angles who fight for God.

God placed everyone on earth to be the same, everyone has their own brain and thoughts. Try to use your brains to better yourselves with kindness and love and stop all this madness in the name of God.

These younger kids of today have no morals at all. They are the evil ones telling all the older people what is right and what needs to be changed in this world. But they do not understand history.

You came into this world alone and you are going out the same way. Peoples' brains are full of hate because they are all spoiled and have no ethics or values.

They think they could follow in the footsteps of great men from the past who changed this world for the better. These younger generations will destroy our country and the world if we do not put a stop to all this nonsense.

We have a bigger agenda to go out and spread the word of God. We will not allow these younger people stand in the way of God.

History always repeats itself in our world. I wish we could just get everyone to understand that we can make life much easier for each other. Now I understand why God wants to destroy this planet.

The hate in this world we live in is all for Satan and the Anti-Christ. We all feed them the power they need to survive in this world. This is why God wants to take Satan's life for good.

He himself gave Satan many chances to repent but, Satan to this day still hates God and everything he does.

People who will not follow Gods rules will perish and never be heard about ever again. I will now end this book with a final notice.

I have work to do in the name of God. I will side with Saint Michael and follow through with what I promised to do for God himself. I will not let ignorance stand in my way.

I will not allow Satan to corrupt my thoughts or with any temptations. I will conduct the will of God. I hope you will all support me in my mission and help spread the word of God. I hope you will pray to God and ask for forgiveness.

I would like all to read what I wrote and start talking about God to others and let's try to start bringing peace toward each other and put a stop to all this hate.

Chapter Nineteen

God loves you all. Try reading the Bible and see for yourselves the power God has. Jesus came to earth and had many followers just by speaking the words from God.

He did not have social media. God let these evil murderers beat and murder his only Son.

Yes, God paid back everyone for what they did back in those days. God has destroyed this world three times before. Yes, he will be destroying it again for the final time.

Because of Satan's evil temptations, God has dealt with hell before. God felt bad having place humans back upon earth with Satan.

He had hopes people would never fall under Satan spells ever again, because of what he gave everyone here on earth.

But he even wished humans had more willpower, and not let temptation carry them in the wrong direction. It would have made Satan weak.

There are no more changes, only because Satan must be destroyed for the good of humanity. God is giving everyone a last chance to give up everything they own and show him you are willing to sacrifice your money and riches and repent to him.

He will know who is real and who is not. I told you all in this book.

You cannot fool God. Everyone must drop to your knees and pray to him. Show him you are willing to give everything back to Satan and refuse to deal with him ever again.

Only then God will hear your confession when you repent to our Father. Everyone will be in a far better place once you leave this place called earth. Never fear dying, for God will accept you into his home if you repent.

Others will be placed elsewhere or turned into dust. Those who did not listen by repenting, I know you will all find out the hard way.

Share your wealth and show your love for once. For God knows and is watching earth more now than ever before. Those who think they can hide money and take it with them are wrong.

God demands they collaborate with what is written by spreading the word of the Lord God.

This is not a request from God, this is what God is Commanding from everyone before the die. They know who they are, they will be afraid to read this book. They must all repent and begs for God's forgiveness.

Many people fear death, and for good reasons. What you really fear is; The Unknown, but they know they did not follow Gods rules here on earth, so they fear.

The only humans should fear the unknown, are the ones who do not believe in God.

Death is nothing to fear for humans, if you believe God is on the other side, there is nothing to worry about.

When Saint Michael comes to destroy this place of evil. People will be in fear of what they will see. No matter what happens here on earth, if you have faith in your higher Power, then never fear dying.

Even Saint Michael told me to tell everyone to show no fear, and just fall to your knees, and say the lords prayers. It will be over in no time for those who pray and have repented.

For those who never listened to me preach the word from God, when I warned them what will happen to this earth. They will die with Satan, and they will never be heard from again, ever.

Just like back in the day when Jesus had warned everyone, nobody wanted to hear what Jesus had to say who was supporting Satan.

Only people who believed in God followed Jesus. Those rich and powerful people can never take their wealth with them. These will be the fools who will challenge God and his will.

People who forgot, and those who never started believing in God, will feel the power of God. Children and adults who laughed and mocked Jesus and his Father, will feel Gods wrath.

Those who do not believe will stay alive long enough and see the destruction on this planet, then they will burn slowly into ash and never be seen ever again.

For this is Gods will. When your life ends, you must have God and love in your hearts and within your soul.

You must make an amends with the people you hate and pray to God. Nobody on this earth has ever followed the commandments written by God. He understands why humans could not follow these simple rules.

His son Jesus was the only one to do this, because God created him perfect. God created man and women in his own image. God knows there are many nonbelievers on this earth who will be punished.

This is why they will have only one chance to pray to him and repent to him from here on. Those who read the Bible try to interpret it in many ways.

Those who turn and twist the words into other people's minds are sinners. They know this, yet they still do this to the weak-minded people every day to take their money.

Bibles have different meaning. Only because they were written by many different authors from back in the days of Jesus. God wants you all to understand, it was all meant to be this way.

There are many different religions on this earth and God looks down and see many religions fight over each other's belief's.

This is wrong, God, is the Almighty, Jesus is his Son, and the Holy Spirit comes between all and is one voice.

The Holy Spirit is like a lifeline between humans and the high Heavens; it keeps the spirit alive, and God's Heven and God himself protects the Holy Spirit.

There are 4200 different religions on this planet, but there is only one God. Remember this, he hears all. The Holy Spirit is everywhere all the time. It is a Trinity.

The Father "God," The Son "Jesus," and the "Holy Spirit" are all three in one. Which many followers know.

Most people speak of their definitions from the Bible within a group and then decide, if it is not their way of thinking, they must fight or kill each other until one side wins.

This is so wrong. You can take many paragraphs from any Good Book and believe whether it's right or wrong.

Authors who wrote the Bible, left so much out of the Bible from back in the days Saint Michael told me. Many good books can be interpreted in so many ways. This was not what God wanted.

God wanted everyone to know one thing. That when you die, you will understand everything before you even meet him.

As your soul travels, you will have every question answered before you meet your Father.

This is why the human brain stays alive about nine minutes longer after their heart stops.

God wanted me to remind everyone that the most powerful person on this earth right now is the Anti-Christ.

He has grown with power from the wars and sinners of this earth. He is an extraordinarily rich and powerful man. This person starts wars and sits back and smiles as humans kill each other.

Most of the rich and powerful people on our earth are demons in their own little ways, and they are corrupt and most know each other.

But with each sin they commit, they grow with more power here on earth. They send out demons using temptation every second of time within humans. This is why God feels the time has come that this world will end.

People have not changed, and they never will. It's because by them being human, and by Satan living amongst humans, this can never work. Satan must be destroyed for the last time. For this is the will of God.

Everyone on earth will be given one warning to "Repent" because Saint Michael will return to this earth and earth will be no more.

Most humans will be saved and those forgiven will start new life in other places. Where they will find love within themselves, and have a good relationship with others, and they will never fear anything, or have any worries.

They will see their loved ones again and stay happy forever. For this is Gods will.

So, please to all who read this one book. Please repent to God. Do not let greed and money take your souls. All this money and whatever you think is valuable is all worthless.

Please tell all your friends of what you just read, and please ask them to start praying to God and repent to him every day. Everything I have told you in this novel is true. I am a sinner telling everyone living on this planet what will happen.

This is not one lie in his book, and I hope you all take this seriously. If you do not, then you will see for yourself for what I have told you will be true. God will never allow you into his place of Heaven.

Life is not a game; people have broken every rule and has forgotten about God. He is not happy. Yet, he still sends word through Saint Michael that he loves you all.

I guess I will find the rest of my answers when I meet him. We have done some good things down here on this place called earth. God has a sense of humor, and he feels most humans still have a lot of good in them.

Just remember this whether you believe this story or not. God is great, kind, and good. He could have come in and taken out earth anytime he wanted without noticing. Why is he placing everyone on notice, I do not know.

When he sent Jesus on this earth, he knew what would happen.

And we all know the outcome of what happen with Jesus, the Son of God. God is giving every person one last chance to believe in him and his Son before destroying this planet. I do hope to see my old friends again, my family and all the pets I've owned.

Death does take a toll on the living. Trust in what you believe, and you will never fear death.

People work hard and I understand the bills that pile up. This world is falling apart. If you cannot see it, then you must be blind. God has been trying to send many messages down here to earth in many ways, but nobody sees them.

Because everyone is too blind to see the truth of what is to come. People have way too much hate within themselves.

Take all that hate and turn it into love. Love will conquer all, It always has. There is no better feeling in this world than to love each other.

God shows signs when people cannot see the truth looking right at them. This novel should be your awakening. Get yourself ready to stand before God almighty himself. All I can do is bring you the message from an Angel.

I wrote this novel in 2020, and this is the year 2025. Many terrible things has happen in our world. On the following pages I would like to share a few prays for you all to say to God.

I am sure once people start buying this novel and pray to the lord thy God, it would make him incredibly happy knowing and showing him how we all love him so much.

Do it from your home if you need to, he will forgive you for all your sins. But like I stated in the beginning of this book. Do not try to fool God

God is waiting for us; you were born on this earth for a reason. Fear nothing and go on your journey and live your life. You were put on this earth for a reason, and you must figure it out.

This is why so many humans have this feeling they were here before, or they did this before, It is because you have.

God wanted you all to live on this earth and not let Satan use his temptation on you.

If you can do this, then you will enter Heaven. Remember this ~ God made all humans not to be perfect. You were all born into this world not knowing anything.

Everything was to be taught to you as you grew.

At some point in your life, each person knows right from wrong. Every human knew or heard about their higher power.

This is why you become who "you" are. This is a fact! This world will see much confusion and chaos between the years 2020 and 2062.

In 2032 over one hundred million Americans will be out of work just in this country. Millions of people will suffer in this world which you all have brought down on yourselves.

The weather will turn for the worse, earthquakes will be stronger, hurricanes will be up to categories seven up to nine and tornados will rip tall buildings down to sand in big cities. In 2062 dust will be filling this planet from Yellowstone Park.

An excessively big Rock will be tossed to Earth once again by the high Heavens.

This you will all know as an (Asteroid). Behind it will be Saint Michael and many Angels to destroy this world for good. Like I said, it has been done many times before. God has killed people and took out cities.

This is why people believed in God and the power he has. God took his son to heaven and to this day Jesus has learned about humans and Satan.

But please try not to sin. Try to be the absolute best a human could be and help people in need.

When you walk by someone in the store, look right at them and say hello to them, trust me, they will say hello in return. Remember God did not make Humans Perfect, you are all here for one reason, figure it out.

Remember you will all die and meet your maker.

This world will be destroyed in November on the 15th day of that month, and the year will be 2062.

Keep God in your life before you die, that is the key to living and dying, you will understand everything when you die and stand before God.

Help me spread the word of God and start acting right. Love the people around you. Stop all the fighting and wars. Because the end is coming, and nobody can stop it from happening.

Just pray each day, confess to God every day, and get all the hate out of your souls.

Trust me, if you all want to meet up with the loved ones you lost, just do what has been asked of you to do in this novel. God be with you all.

Death: I will be gone before many of you. Everything I did, I did for God. Only God can judge me, not any human. I am not worried about what any human thinks of me, because only God can judge.

Death is an irreversible process. Where one loses their existence as a human being. Your soul will go right to an Angel, and you will be brought right before God Almighty himself. Then be judged for what you have done on this place called earth.

In the past God had sent you all back here to earth just to see if you can get it right to enter heaven. God is a very forgiving, remember that.

God loves each one of his children. This is why he is giving everyone notice of what is coming your way. You are all going to die, and this planet will be no more.

He expects all believers to come forth and help me out by spreading the word of God.

The worst things that will start happening in this world will be with the weather. God will be sending you all a message. Just to show you what is coming your way.

God is not a monster. God is pure Love. I get this feeling that comes over me when he is near me, trust in God. Thank you all for reading this message. "It's always calm before the storm" Remember this…

It is important to recognize that humanity does not exist in isolation on Earth. The answers to our inquiries regarding both our history and our future are readily accessible to each one of us.

Also, death is the only way any human can leave this planet. No human has ever been of this planet, let me make this very clear. All those satellites up in our skies are just above the earths atmosphere, this is as far as any human can go.

All the answers are in our oceans; I laugh when all these scientists talk about the Big Bang Theory. The human body is one remarkable system. God created all of us because we are made perfect. People are followers and humans need to follow their own beliefs when it comes to God.

Help me get the word out there. I want nothing in return; Everyone must start to believe in their higher power. You are all on Notice!!!

God Bless!

Final Chapter

~ The Lords Pray; Our Father in heaven, hallowed be your name. Your kingdom comes, your will be done, on earth as it is in heaven. Give us our daily bread this day, and forgive us our debts, as we also have forgiven our debtors. And lead us not into temptation but deliver us from evil.

~ The Hail Mary Pray Hail Mary, Full of Grace, The Lord is with thee. Blessed art thou among women and blessed is the fruit of thy womb Jesus. Holy Mary, Mother of God, pray for us sinners now, and at the hour of death. Glory Be to the Father, and to the Son, and to the Holy Spirit.

~ Guardian Angel Prayer: Angel of God, my guardian dear to whom God's love commits me here, ever this day be at my side, to light and guard to rule and guide.

~ Amen Glory Be to the Father ~ Prayers Glory be to the Father and to the Son and to the Holy Spirit. As it was in the beginning is now, and ever shall be, a world without end.

~ Before you Eat, Lord God, Heavenly Father. This meal is the work of your hands. You have provided it for me, again, and I am grateful. bless us and these Thy gifts which we receive from Thy bountiful goodness, through Jesus Christ, our Lord.

~ Sign of the Cross Prayer: The sign of the cross is a prayer, a blessing, and sacramental. As a sacramental, it prepares an individual to receive grace and disposes one to cooperate with it. The Christian begins the day, prayers, and activities with the Sign of the Cross: "In the name of the Father and of the Son and of the Holy Spirit.

~ A Prayer of Confession; Father, I confess my tendency to forget to ask your blessing upon my life, through the comforts that you have given me to enjoy. So many people lack these daily comforts, and it is selfish of me to forget about them in their need. Show me how to make the most of Your blessing in my life, for everything I have is a gift from You. In Jesus' Name.

I love you all ~ GOD! "This book has been blessed for all who read it."

"Please spread the word of God and let us all try to have a good relationship with each other. Find peace with your heart and it will reach your soul...

Michaelmckay712@yahoo.com

Website: michaelmckaybostonauthor.com

www.ingramcontent.com/pod-product-compliance
Lightning Source LLC
Chambersburg PA
CBHW071526150726
48000CB00002B/694